Time I Am -4

# Lost Time

## Is Never Found Again

By
Dr. Sahadeva dasa

B.com., FCA., AICWA., PhD
Chartered Accountant

Soul Science University Press

www.TimeIAm.com

Readers interested in the subject matter of this
book are invited to correspond with the publisher at:
SoulScienceUniversity@gmail.com   +91 98490 95990
or visit DrDasa.com


First Edition: February 2014


Soul Science University Press expresses its gratitude to the
Bhaktivedanta Book Trust International (BBT), for the use of quotes by
His Divine Grace A.C.Bhaktivedanta Swami Prabhupada.

ISBN 978-93-82947-10-3


Published by:
Dr. Sahadeva dasa for Soul Science University Press


Printed by:
Rainbow Print Pack, Hyderabad


To order a copy write to purnabramhadasa@gmail.com
or buy online: Amazon.com, rlbdeshop.com

# By The Same Author

*Oil–Final Countdown To A Global Crisis And Its Solutions*

*End of Modern Civilization And Alternative Future*

*To Kill Cow Means To End Human Civilization*

*Cow And Humanity – Made For Each Other*

*Cows Are Cool – Love 'Em!*

*Let's Be Friends – A Curious, Calm Cow*

*Wondrous Glories of Vraja*

*We Feel Just Like You Do*

*Tsunami Of Diseases Headed Our Way – Know Your Food Before Time Runs Out*

*Cow Killing And Beef Export – The Master Plan To Turn India Into A Desert By 2050*

*Capitalism Communism And Cowism – A New Economics For The 21st Century*

*Noble Cow – Munching Grass, Looking Curious And Just Hanging Around*

*World – Through The Eyes Of Scriptures*

*To Save Time Is To Lengthen Life*

*Life Is Nothing But Time – Time Is Life, Life Is Time*

*An Inch of Time Can Not Be Bought With A Mile of Gold*

*Spare Us Some Carcasses – An Appeal From The Vultures*

*Cow Dung – A Down-To- Earth Solution To Global Warming And Climate Change*

*Cow Dung For Food Security And Survival of Human Race*

(More information on availability on DrDasa.com )

# Contents

# Preface

Time needs your tender loving care because it is a unique, irreplaceable resource. Taking it for granted would be your undoing. Time is not found on supermarkets shelves in case you need an extra supply. There are no vending machines even. There is no place where you can buy or hire extra time. Neither you can pull it out from the last year's stock. As the Sun sets on the horizon, your day is gone and as the Sun rises in the east, your night is gone. Gone means gone forever, never to return. There are many things in life which go and come back but time is not one of those.

When something is in short supply, you look for a substitute. Everything in the world has a substitute except time. Nothing can replace time or take its place.

Time is a universal ingredient. Everything requires time. Here again there are no exceptions, no shortcuts. Everything is produced in time, stays in time and perishes in time.

Time is cruel. It shows no mercy. When time is up, it's up.

A poet says,

This thing all things devours

Birds, beasts, trees, flowers

Gnaws iron, bites steel,
Grinds hard stones to meal,
Slays king, ruins town,
And beats high mountain down!

Respect the sheer power of time. And do it before your time's up.

*Sahadeva dasa*

Dr. Sahadeva dasa
1st April 2014
Secunderabad, India

# A Note On The Book Format

This book is based on One Victory A Day™ format. The chapters are arranged date wise. A reader need not read the book serially. He can open any chapter and he will find something useful for the day.

According to surveys, 80% of the books bought don't get read beyond 10% of their contents. They just sit in the shelves. This is especially true in recent times.

The thickness of the book acts as a deterrent, especially due to lack of time. Desperation grows and book lands in the shelf.

In One Victory A Day™ format, the book need not be completed. The idea is to read the chapter related to the day, and then understand, digest, assimilate and implement the information. That is improving life in small measures or changing life one day at a time. Throughout the day, you can try to reflect on and implement the newfound information.

Most of the books bought are not read fully because the reader can not relate the information to his or her life. Purpose of knowledge is not entertainment but betterment of life. Purpose of information is transformation, otherwise it's a waste of time. Ingestion of information without assimilation is like intake of food without digestion.

To scale a highrise, we go up one step at a time. To finish our meal, we eat one morsel at a time. A skyscraper is constructed one brick at a time. And an ocean is nothing but an assembly of many drops. This is the power of small. A big target, when broken down into small steps, becomes easily attainable.

People who are not into reading should cultivate the habit of reading in small installments. Phenomenal achievements can be accomplished by consistent and daily improvements. Good reading is as essential as clean air and water. Anything done regularly becomes a habit.

The mind's garden will produce whatever we sow in it. Daily we are being bombarded with a massive dose of undesirable information. The only way to counteract it is through assimilation of desirable information.

Nido Qubein's says, "One of the greatest resources people cannot mobilize themselves is that they try to accomplish great things. Most worthwhile achievements are the result of many little things done in a single direction."

April 1

# Atomic Time To Universal Time

## Divisions And Subdivisions

I n ancient India, there were elaborate formulae for calculation
of time. Vedic cosmological accounts confirm to modern
scientific findings. In Vedic system, smallest unit of time is atomic
time and calculations are expanded upto the time of this universe's
existence.

Srimad Bhagavatam defines atom as the material manifestation's
ultimate particle, which is indivisible and not formed into a body.

This atomic description of the Srimad-Bhāgavatam is almost the
same as the recently discovered atomic theory and this is further
described in the Paramanu-vada of Kanada. In modern science also,
the atom is accepted as the ultimate indivisible particle of which
the universe is composed.

*Time is the coin of your life. It is the only coin you have, and only you
can determine how it will be spent. Be careful lest you let other people
spend it for you.*     ~ Carl Sandburg

11

One can estimate time by measuring the movement of the atomic combination of bodies. Time and space are two correlative terms. Time is measured in terms of its covering a certain space of atoms.

Standard time is calculated in terms of the movement of the sun. The time covered by the sun in passing over an atom is calculated as atomic time. The greatest time of all covers the entire existence of the nondual manifestation. All the planets rotate and cover space, and space is calculated in terms of atoms. Each planet has its particular orbit for rotating, in which it moves without deviation, and similarly the sun has its orbit. The complete calculation of the time of creation, maintenance and dissolution, measured in terms of the circulation of the total planetary systems until the end of creation, is known as the supreme kala or the supreme time.

The division of gross time is calculated as follows: two atoms make one double atom, and three double atoms make one hexatom. This hexatom is visible in the sunshine which enters through the holes of a window screen.

The atom is described as an invisible particle, but when six such atoms combine together, they are called a trasarenu, and this is visible in the sunshine pouring through the holes of a window screen.

The time duration needed for the integration of three trasarenus is called a truti, and one hundred trutis make one vedha. Three vedhas make one lava.

It is calculated that if a second is divided into 1687.5 parts, each part is the duration of a truti, which is the time occupied in the integration of eighteen atomic particles. Such a combination of atoms into different bodies creates the calculation of material time. The sun is the central point for calculating all different durations.

The duration of time of three lavas is equal to one nimesa, the combination of three nimesas makes one ksana, five ksanas combined together make one kastha, and fifteen kasthas make one laghu.

Fifteen laghus make one nadika, which is also called a danda. Two dandas make one muhurta, and six or seven dandas make one fourth of a day or night, according to human calculation.

Now as per vedic system, the measuring pot for one nadika, or danda, can be prepared with a six-pala-weight [fourteen ounce] pot of copper, in which a hole is bored with a gold probe weighing four masa and measuring four fingers long. When the pot is placed on water, the time before the water overflows in the pot is called one danda.

It is advised herein that the bore in the copper measuring pot must be made with a probe weighing not more than four masa and measuring not longer than four fingers. This regulates the diameter of the hole. The pot is submerged in water, and the overflooding time is called a danda. This is another way of measuring the duration of a danda, just as time is measured by sand in a glass. It appears that in the days of Vedic civilization there was no dearth of knowledge in physics, chemistry or higher mathematics. Measurements were calculated in different ways, as simply as could be done.

It is calculated that there are four praharas, which are also called yamas, in the day and four in the night of the human being. Similarly, fifteen days and nights are a fortnight, and there are two fortnights, white and black, in a month.

The aggregate of two fortnights is one month, and that period is one complete day and night for the Pita planets. Two of such months comprise one season, and six months comprise one complete movement of the sun from south to north.

Two solar movements make one day and night of the demigods, and that combination of day and night is one complete calendar year for the human being. The human being has a duration of life of one hundred years.

Influential stars, planets, luminaries and atoms all over the universe are rotating in their respective orbits under the direction of the Supreme, represented by eternal kala.

In the Brahma-samhita it is stated that the sun is the eye of the Supreme and it rotates in its particular orbit of time. Similarly, beginning from the sun down to the atom, all bodies are under the influence of the kala-chakra, or the orbit of eternal time, and each of them has a scheduled orbital time of one samvatsara.

Following is a table of vedic timings in terms of the modern clock.

| | | | |
|---|---|---|---|
| One truti | - | 8/13,500 | second |
| One vedha | - | 8/135 | second |
| One lava | - | 8/45 | second |
| One nimesa | - | 8/15 | second |
| One ksana | - | 8/5 | second |
| One kastha | - | 8 | seconds |
| One laghu | - | 2 | minutes |
| One danda | - | 30 | minutes |
| One prahara | - | 3 | hours |
| One day | - | 12 | hours |
| One night | - | 12 | hours |
| One paksa | - | 15 | days |
| One year | - | 365 | days |
| 432,000 years | - | Kali-yuga | |
| 864,000 years. | - | Dvapara-yuga | |
| 1,296,000 years | - | Treta-yuga | |
| 1,728,000 years | - | Satya-yuga | |
| 4,320,000 years | - | Divya-yuga (Aggregate of 4 yugas) | |
| 1000 Divya-yugas | - | 12 hours ((One day)of Lord Brahma | |

365 Days & Nights - 1 year of Lord Brahma

100 years of Brahma - Life of the universe or breathing period of the Supreme Lord

The entire duration of the life of Brahmä is calculated to be less than a second of the Lord's time, and it is explained in the Brahma-samhita (5.48) as follows:

"I worship Govinda, the Supreme Personality of Godhead, the cause of all causes, whose plenary portion is Maha-Visnu. All the heads of the innumerable universes [the Brahmas] live only by taking shelter of the time occupied by one of His breaths."

This is the description of the measurements of time, beginning from the smallest fraction measured by the movement of a single atom up to the total life span of the universe, as described by Sukadeva Goswami to King Pariksit in Srimad Bhagavatam.

Reference:

Srimad Bhagavatam, Canto 3, Chapter 11, A.C.Bhaktivedanta Swami Prabhupada, BBTI.

*The sun-god, who is Narayana, or Visnu, the soul of all the worlds, is situated in outer space between the upper and lower portions of the universe. Passing through twelve months on the wheel of time, the sun comes in touch with twelve different signs of the zodiac and assumes twelve different names according to those signs. The aggregate of those twelve months is called a samvatsara, or an entire year. According to lunar calculations, two fortnights—one of the waxing moon and the other of the waning—form one month. That same period is one day and night for the planet Pitrloka. According to stellar calculations, a month equals two and one quarter constellations. When the sun travels for two months, a season passes, and therefore the seasonal changes are considered parts of the body of the year.*

# Monetary Value

## of Time

A man came home from work late, tired and irritated, to find his 5-year old son waiting for him at the door.

"Daddy, may I ask you a question?"

"Yes sure, what is it?" replied the man

"Daddy, how much do you make an hour?"

"That's none of your business," the man replied angrily.

"I just want to know, please tell me", pleaded the little boy.

"If you must know, I make Rs.100 an hour"

"Oh," the little boy replied, with his head down. Then looking up, he said, "Dad, may I please borrow Rs.50?"

The father was furious, "I work long hard hours everyday and don't have time for fooling around with you."

After a bit of cooling down, "It's been a long day son. Here's Rs.50 you asked for."

The little boy was all perked up and then, reaching under his pillow he pulled out some old bills.

The little boy slowly counted out his money, and then looked up at his father.

"Why did you want money when you already had some?" the father grumbled.

"Because I didn't have enough, but now I do," the little boy replied.

"Daddy, I have Rs.100 now, can I buy an hour of your time one of these days?"

Reference:
Divya.K.Swamy, Chennai

*This morning I was telling the story of a son asking his mother, "Who is this man?" He was his father, and he had never seen. "You have seen father." No, rather, he had no chance to see father because when the father comes back from the office it is night, ten o'clock or more than that. That time the son is sleeping, and again he has to go early in the morning. That time also, son is sleeping. So he did not know. So one Sunday, when he's grown up, he is asking his mother, "Who is this man?" "So this man..." Not only in India, everywhere. I have seen in New York from the other island? What is that?*

*Hamsaduta: Long Island.*

*Prabhupada: Long Island. They are coming two hours in the ferry, three hours in the bus. They are going to the office. Eight hours there. Then five hours and eight hours, thirteen hours, again five hours. Then thirteen and..., eighteen hours. And for six hours they have got home. "Home sweet home."*

*Mahamsa: I knew people coming from Poona to Bombay to work.*
*(Room Conversation -- December 12, 1976, Hyderabad)*

## Power Of Small Things

### The Devil Is In The Detail

A person took some friends out to a new restaurant, and noticed that the waiter who took their order carried a spoon in his shirt pocket.

It seemed a little strange.

When the busboy brought their water and utensils, he noticed he also had a spoon in his shirt pocket. Then he looked around and saw that all the staff had spoons in their pockets.

When the waiter came back to serve their soup he asked, "Why the spoon?"

"Well," he explained, "the restaurant's owners hired Andersen Consulting to revamp all our processes. After several months of analysis, they concluded that the spoon was the most frequently dropped utensil. It represents a drop in frequency of approximately

3 spoons per table per hour. If our personnel are better prepared, we can reduce the number of trips back to the kitchen and save 15 man-hours per shift."

The way we do small things determines the way we do everything.

As luck would have it, the person dropped his spoon and the waiter was able to replace it with his spare. "I'll get another spoon next time I go to the kitchen instead of making an extra trip to get it right now."

If 15 minutes are saved per waiter per day by this exercise, it adds up to 90 hours per year per waiter. That's a saving of more than 2 weeks of work per year per waiter.

> *Life is so valuable that we cannot waste even a second without any profit. That is the aim of life. The materialist persons, especially in country like yours, they calculate... I do not know. When I was in India I heard it that if you go to see an important businessman, his secretary, while talking with that man, the secretary gives you a card that "This Mr. such and such cannot spare more than two minutes." Is it a fact? Anyway, we should not waste our time, either you act materially or spiritually.*
> *~ Srila Prabhupada (Srimad Bhagavatam 7.6.6 -- New Vrindaban, June 22, 1976)*

# Killing Time

## A Hyper-Active, Hyper-Consuming Society

by Wendy Richmond

I was on a full plane, and we had already been sitting on the tarmac for ages when the pilot announced that it would be at least 45 minutes before we would get off the ground. You can imagine the collective groan.

But then he said, "You can turn your cell phones on." The sudden burst of energy was like a bunch of kids just let out of school. The pilot had released us from unbearable confinement: the prison of inactivity. In the following half hour, I'll bet that more than a hundred phone calls were sent and received. I eavesdropped on the calls closest to me, and it seemed as though most consisted of chatting with family members or friends.

This was a planeload of people who were simultaneously engaged in the exercise of killing time.

In our twenty-first century society, most of us have lives that consist of densely packed activities. We do so many different things in different locations with different people (even when we are just sitting at our computers) that we have created a by-product, innumerable "in-between" spaces of time. They are the gaps that exist between finishing one thing and starting the next: the time between arriving at the doctor's office and being examined;

between descending into the subway station and the train's arrival; between the barista asking, "What drink may I start for you?" and announcing, "grande non-fat vanilla latte."

These gaps are typically short and unpredictable in length, empty moments that, for the most part, simply require us to wait.

But we never simply "wait," do we?

Because we are a hyper-active, hyper-consuming society, we have to be busy, productive and entertained, even during the in-betweens. Nature abhors a vacuum, and so empty spaces must be filled. To answer that need, we have created, and are consumers of, entire new industries for killing time.

There have always been industries that have served short bouts of waiting, even when the primary business is something else. Restaurants, bars and cafes, for example, are for dining and hanging out. But the Starbucks on every corner is also a provider of a little something extra to do--i.e., sipping coffee--while you're waiting on a subway platform.

What interests me most is how many new ways there are to kill time, brought to us by new technology. The product requirements include speed, portability and the ability to be interrupted at a moment's notice. They are mini devices for mini activities. Or they need to be imbedded in "smart" places where waiting occurs— airport terminals, bus stops, hotel lobbies—where you can kill time more effectively, enjoyably and knowledgeably.

I travel a lot and much of my waiting takes place at airports. Lately, I have been observing my time-killing habits more closely, taking care to notice how technology industries are providing products and services--intentionally or not—to fill the vacuum.

My mini activities fall roughly into three categories: shopping, entertainment and productivity.

### Shopping

Let's start with the mother of all mini activities: shopping. The airline terminals are filled with shops, becoming more and more like malls with chain stores for jewelry, clothing and souvenirs. Plus there are stores that supply paraphernalia for your flight, along with books and magazines, you can buy batteries, DVDs, CDs, headphones and other peripherals for your time-killing technology devices.

Or you can go to the Wi-Fi hot spots and continue to shop, but use your computer. When I have miraculously passed quickly through security and now have extra time (to kill), I peruse the books at the airport news stores and, disappointed, I go online to purchase and download a song or a podcast. A crucial goal for a time-killing business is to sell more stuff more quickly. Every time I go to Amazon, there are new, targeted suggestions for additional purchases. Filling out the forms is lightning fast, because almost all of my contact and billing information is stored.

Last year I bought a bracelet at an airport store. The salesperson took forever to ring it up. I muttered to myself, "I could have done this faster online." But then I realized it didn't really matter. I never wear bracelets anyway, and I still haven't worn the one I bought that day. I just bought it because I needed something to do.

### Entertainment

It's interesting to see how the cell phones are changing. "Your mobile phone will be with you at all times, filled with digital content that is both trivial and vital, from your 'to do' list to the details of your identity: e-mail, Internet access and instant messaging; movie information (with directions and options to purchase tickets); music and podcasts; games and television shows; news, weather and stock quotes. These are in addition to the phone's cameras (still and video), appointment book, address book, music and video players..." All of these features serve as ideal time fillers, especially the last one: video players. Have you heard the phrase "fourth screen"? The mobile telephone is becoming the fourth screen in our everyday lives, the first three being the cinema screen, the TV and the computer.

In this way, mobile phones will be used for video snacking. But do I really want to snack on more junk TV, even to kill a few minutes? This made me think about independent filmmakers, so I Googled the phrase "independent filmmakers on cell phones." From that cursory search, it's clear that I will have a lot of new choices for filling three minutes while I wait to board the plane.

### Productivity

Many people are desperate to be productive during waiting periods, and they accomplish a great deal with short spurts of e-mail, text messaging, Web surfing and phone calls.

My most important device for productive mini activities is my noise-cancelling headphones. You might put these in the entertainment category, for enhancing my music-listening. But for me, they are a necessity for my most desperate need, to kill the time on the tarmac. That "in-between" is when I cannot use my laptop or cell phone (the above pilot-hero scenario is unusual) and when babies tend to scream. Couple that with the exasperation of not moving and having no idea when we will. Call me spoiled, but I find it hard to be productive under those circumstances, and a cocoon of clear, calm music helps me to think.

Inevitably, I come to the chicken-and-egg question. Which comes first, new technology or our need for it? In other words, is technology developed to address our need to kill time more effectively and enjoyably? Or, do we have this desire because of our addiction to, and the effects of, new technology?

I wrote part of this column during a cross-country flight. I took a break to walk up and down the aisle to check out other people's

> *mandasya manda-prajnasya*
> *vayo mandayusas ca vai*
> *nidraya hriyate naktam*
> *diva ca vyartha-karmabhih*
>
> *Lazy human beings with paltry intelligence and a short duration of life pass the night sleeping and the day performing activities that are for naught.*
>
> *The less intelligent do not know the real value of the human form of life. The human form is a special gift of material nature in the course of her enforcing stringent laws of miseries upon the living being. It is a chance to achieve the highest boon of life, namely to get out of the entanglement of repeated birth and death. The intelligent take care of this important gift by strenuously endeavoring to get out of the entanglement. But the less intelligent are lazy and unable to evaluate the gift of the human body to achieve liberation from the material bondage; they become more interested in so-called economic development and work very hard throughout life simply for the sense enjoyment of the temporary body. Sense enjoyment is also allowed to the lower animals by the law of nature, and thus a human being is also destined to a certain amount of sense enjoyment according to his past or present life. But one should definitely try to understand that sense enjoyment is not the ultimate goal of human life. Herein it is said that during the daytime one works "for nothing" because the aim is nothing but sense enjoyment. We can particularly observe how the human being is engaged for nothing in the great cities and industrial towns. There are so many things manufactured by human energy, but they are all meant for sense enjoyment, and not for getting out of material bondage. And after working hard during the daytime, a tired man either sleeps or engages in sex habits at night. That is the program of materialistic civilized life for the less intelligent. Therefore they are designated herein as lazy, unfortunate and short-lived.*
>
> ~ Srimad Bhagavatam 1.16.9

killing time technology--DVD players, iPods, computers, Game Boys, headphones--and then I came upon a young woman who was knitting. Knitting! After I passed her seat, I glanced back and saw a tiny dvd player on her tray table, screen glowing.

Reference

Wendy Richmond© 2007 W. Richmond

# Remember

## Who or What You Work For

A recent UK TV commercial showed short clips of children admonishing their work-obsessed parents.

"Your fired" said the children, as parents came home late from work, or missed special moments.

The ads finished with the statement "remember who you're working for".

Working simply for the sake of work is mode of ignorance. Workaholism is a madnesss.

Ask the questions about the work you do:

What am I doing? - am I doing something that's worth doing, however that may be defined?

Why am I doing it? - what is my ultimate goal or reward?

> *yat karosi yad asnasi*
> *yaj juhosi dadasi yat*
> *yat tapasyasi kaunteya*
> *tat kurusva mad-arpanam*
>
> *Whatever you do, whatever you eat, whatever you offer or give away, and whatever austerities you perform -- do that, O son of Kunti, as an offering to Me.*
>
> *~ Krishna (Bhagavad gita 9.27)*

Who am I doing it for? - for myself, families, others? If you are confused about the answers to these questions, you may be suffering from workaholism. A workaholic is a person who is addicted to work. The term generally implies that the persons enjoys their work; it can also imply that they simply feel compelled to do it. There is no generally accepted medical definition of such a condition, although some forms of stress, impulse control disorder, obsessive-compulsive personality disorder can be work-related.

*The typical example of the beast of burden is the ass. This humble beast is made to work very hard by his master. The ass does not really know for whom he works so hard day and night. He remains satisfied by filling his stomach with a bundle of grass, sleeping for a while under fear of being beaten by his master, and satisfying his sex appetite at the risk of being repeatedly kicked by the opposite party. The ass sings poetry and philosophy sometimes, but this braying sound only disturbs others. This is the position of the foolish fruitive worker who does not know for whom he should work. He does not know that karma (action) is meant for yajna (sacrifice).*

*Most often, those who work very hard day and night to clear the burden of self-created duties say that they have no time to hear of the immortality of the living being. To such mudhas, material gains, which are destructible, are life's all in all-despite the fact that the mudhas enjoy only a very small fraction of the fruit of labor. Sometimes they spend sleepless days and nights for fruitive gain, and although they may have ulcers or indigestion, they are satisfied with practically no food; they are simply absorbed in working hard day and night for the benefit of illusory masters. Ignorant of their real master, the foolish workers waste their valuable time serving mammon. Unfortunately, they never surrender to the supreme master of all masters, nor do they take time to hear of Him from the proper sources. The swine who eat the night soil do not care to accept sweetmeats made of sugar and ghee. Similarly, the foolish worker will untiringly continue to hear of the sense-enjoyable tidings of the flickering mundane world, but will have very little time to hear about the eternal living force that moves the material world.*

*~ Srila Prabhupada (Bhagavad gita - 7.15)*

Workaholism in Japan is considered a serious social problem leading to early death, often on the job, a phenomenon dubbed karoshi. Overwork was popularly blamed for the fatal stroke of Prime Minister of Japan Keizō Obuchi, in the year 2000.

In the U.S. and Canada, workaholism remains what it's always been: the so-called "respectable addiction" that's dangerous as any other.

## Manage Your Monkeys

An interesting book on time management is: The One Minute Manager Meets the Monkey by Kenneth Blanchard.

The point of the story is that you can't manage time if you don't manage the monkey. The monkeys are problems that come to you during the day which take up your time. If you start managing other people's monkeys, you will have no time for your own.

For instance, (and you can use this for any situation, not just business) if my employee walks into my office with a monkey (problem) on his back, the monkey is completely his. If he says to me, "hey boss, "WE" have a problem", then the monkey jumps partially off his shoulder and puts one leg on my shoulder.

Now we both have a problem. (Problems = time spent on fixing them). If I say, well tell me about your problem, I am really saying, take some of my time away from spending on my stuff and spend on your stuff.

Once I do this, the monkey leans more on my shoulder than my employee's and I am now spending more time on the problem than he is.

If I say, OK, let me look at this for a while and get back to you, then the monkey has completely jumped on my shoulder. This means that I have to spend time on someone else's stuff rather than my own. BUT, if I say, well come up with some ideas and get back to me with them and we will see if you need help at that time....then the monkey goes completely back on my employee's shoulder and I am free to do my own stuff and manage my own monkeys.

You can relate this to your personal experience when someone gives you a problem to deal with which is really their's in the first place. You, instead of empowering them to do it themselves, end up spending your precious emotional and physical energy on someone else's problem while you have enough to deal with in your own backyard. Or you have gotten between two people and helped mediate an issue when it isn't your problem to begin with.

# There Ain't No Such Thing As A Free Lunch

Everything In Life Requires Time And Efforts

'There ain't no such thing as a free lunch' (alternatively, "There's no such thing as a free lunch.") is a popular adage communicating the idea that it is impossible to get something for nothing.

Uses of the phrase dating back to the 1930s and 1940s have been found, but the phrase's first appearance is unknown.

The free-market economist Milton Friedman popularized the phrase by using it as the title of a 1975 book, and it often appears in economics textbooks. Campbell McConnell writes that the idea is "at the core of economics".

The "free lunch" refers to the once-common tradition of saloons in the United States providing a "free" lunch to patrons who had purchased at least one drink. Many foods on offer were high in salt (e.g., ham, cheese and salted crackers), so those who ate them ended up buying a lot of beer.

Rudyard Kipling, writing in 1891, noted how he

"...came upon a bar room full of bad Salon pictures, in which men with hats on the backs of their heads were wolfing food from a counter. It was the institution of the 'free lunch' I had struck. You paid for a drink and got as much as you wanted to eat. For something less than a dollar a day a man can feed himself sumptuously in San Francisco, even though he be a bankrupt. Remember this if ever you are stranded in these parts."

This phrase indicates an acknowledgement that in reality a person or a society cannot get "something for nothing". Even if something appears to be free, there is always a cost to the person or to society as a whole, although that may be a hidden cost or an externality. For example, a bar offering a free lunch will likely charge more for its drinks.

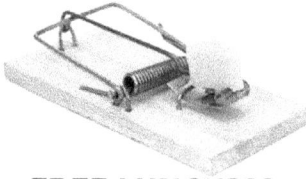

Greg Mankiw described the concept as follows: "To get one thing that we like, we usually have to give up another thing that we like. Making decisions requires trading off one goal against another."

**FREE LUNCH???**

In the sciences, this phrase means that the universe as a whole is ultimately a closed system. There is no magic source of matter, energy, light, or indeed lunch, that does not draw resources from something else, and that will not eventually be exhausted. Therefore the phrase may also be applied to natural physical processes in a

---

*niyatam kuru karma tvam*
*karma jyayo hy akarmanah*
*sarira-yatrapi ca te*
*na prasiddhyed akarmanah*
*Perform your prescribed duty, for doing so is better than not working.*
*One cannot even maintain one's physical body without work.*
*~ Krishna (Bhagavad gita 3.8)*

closed system (either the universe as a whole, or any system that does not receive energy or matter from outside).

In life, there are no shortcuts. There is no alternative to sincere hard work. Material world is designed is a way that one has to work.

There is a story. A crow was sitting on a tree, doing nothing all day. A small rabbit saw the crow, and asked him, "Can I also sit like you and do nothing all day long?"

The crow answered: "Sure, why not." So, the rabbit sat on the ground below the crow, and rested. All of a sudden, a fox appeared, jumped on the rabbit and ate it.

To sit and do nothing, you must be sitting very, very high up.

*This is the material world. As soon as you get some profit here, another side loss. As soon as you want to construct a big skyscraper, another side, digging earth. (laughter) Otherwise, where you get? You cannot create. The stones and bricks, you cannot create. You have to dig from somewhere else and pile here. And that is advancement of civilization, to be engaged in digging and piling. (laughter) This is called advancement of civilization. The rascals, they do not think, "Why, uselessly, I am digging and piling? After all, maya will kick me out, and there will (be) no more digging and piling." But they are very much busy. They cannot come to hear Bhagavad-gita. They are very busy. This is called maya.*
*~ Srila Prabhupada (Bhagavad-gita 2.13 -- Germany, June 18,*

## Learn To Say "No"

Learning to say no is an essential social skill. It is good to help others but it not good to spread out yourself too thinly. People can make incessant demand on your resources. But even if you give away your whole life, people will not be satisfied. No one has succeeded in people-pleasing so far. Check out the story of the donkey, the miller and his son. No matter how they walked, people commented on the miller and his son.

People-pleasers want everyone around them to be happy and they will do whatever is asked of them to keep it that way.

They put everyone else before themselves. For some, saying "yes" is a habit; for others, it's almost an addiction that makes them feel like they need to be needed. This makes them feel important and like they're "contributing to someone else's life."

People-pleasers yearn for outside validation. Their "personal feeling of security and self-confidence is based on getting the approval of others," sayd Linda Tillman, Ph.D, a clinical psychologist in Atlanta. Thus, at the core, people-pleasers lack confidence.

They worry how others will view them when they say no. People don't want to be seen as lazy, uncaring, selfish or totally egocentric.

They fear "they'll be disliked and cut from the group," whether it's friends, family or co-workers.

What many people-pleasers don't realize is that people-pleasing can have serious risks. Not only does it put a lot of pressure and stress on you, but essentially you can make yourself sick from doing too much. If you're overcommitted, you probably get less sleep and get more anxious and upset. You're also depleting your energy resources. In the worst case scenario, you'll wake up and find yourself depressed, because you're on such overload because you possibly can't do it all.

### Why We Find It Hard To Say "No"

To learn to say "No", we have to first understand what's resisting us about it. Below are common reasons why people find it hard to say no:

**You want to help** - You are a kind soul at heart. You don't want to turn the person away and you want to help where possible, even if it may eat into your time.

**Afraid of being rude** - Many of us are brought up under the notion that saying "No", especially to people who are more senior, is rude. This thinking is common in Asia culture, where face-saving is important.

**Wanting to be agreeable** - You don't want to alienate yourself from the group because you're not in agreement. So you confirm to others' requests.

**Fear of conflict** - You are afraid the person might be angry if you reject him/her. This might lead to an ugly confrontation. Even if there isn't, there might be dissent created which might lead to negative consequences in the future.

**Fear of lost opportunities** - Perhaps you are worried saying no means closing doors.

Not burning bridges - Some people take "no" as a sign of rejection. It might lead to bridges being burned and relationships severed.

At the end of the day, it's about how you say "no", rather than the fact you're saying no, that affects the outcome. After all, you have your own priorities and needs, just like everyone has his/her own needs. Saying no is about respecting and valuing your time and space. Say no is your prerogative.

### 7 Simple Ways To Say "No"

Rather than avoid it altogether, it's all about learning the right way to say no. Many people, after they begin to say no to others, they realize it's really not as bad as they thought. Really, the fears of saying no are just in our mind.

If you are not sure how to do so, here are 7 simple ways for you to say no. Use the method that best meets your needs in the situation.

**1. "I can't commit to this as I have other priorities at the moment."**

If you are too busy to engage in the request/offer, this will be applicable. This

lets the person know your plate is full at the moment, so he/she should hold off on this as well as future requests. If it makes it easier, you can also share what you're working on so the person can understand better.

**2. "Now's not a good time as I'm in the middle of something. How about we reconnect at X time?"**

It's common to get sudden requests for help when you are in the middle of something. Sometimes you get phone calls from friends or associates when you're in a meeting or doing important work. This method is a great way to (temporarily) hold off the request. First, you let the person know it's not a good time as you are doing something. Secondly, you make known your desire to help by suggesting another time (at your convenience). This way, the person doesn't feel blown off.

**3. "I'd love to do this, but ..."**

It's a gentle way of breaking no to the other party. It's encouraging as it lets the person know you like the idea (of course, only say this if you do like it) and there's nothing wrong about it.

**4. "Let me think about it first and I'll get back to you."**

This is more like a "Maybe" than a straight out "No". If you are interested but you don't want to say 'yes' just yet, use this. If the person is sincere about the request, he/she will be more than happy to wait a short while. Specify a date / time-range (say, in 1-2 weeks) where the person can expect a reply.

**5. "This doesn't meet my needs now but I'll be sure to keep you in mind."**

If someone is pitching a deal/opportunity which isn't what you are looking for, let him/her know straight-out that it doesn't meet your needs. Otherwise, the discussion can drag on longer than it should.

**6. "I'm not the best person to help on this. Why don't you try X?"**

If you are being asked for help in something which you (i) can't contribute much to (ii) don't have resources to help, let it be known they are looking at the wrong person. If possible, refer them to a lead

> *The European and American youths in the Krsna consciousness movement have been accustomed to many bad habits since birth, but now they have given these up. Many people think that it is impossible to live without illicit sex, intoxication, meat-eating and gambling. One famous Marquess told one of my Godbrothers, "Please make me a brahmana." My Godbrother said, "Yes, it is not a very difficult thing. Simply give up these bad habits -- intoxication, illicit sex, meat-eating and gambling. Then you can become a brahmana." The Marquess then said, "Impossible! This is our life." Actually we have seen that in Western countries older men cannot give up these habits, and because of this they are suffering, yet many young boys and girls have given them up, and there is no suffering. This is due to Krsna consciousness.*
>
> ~ *Srila Prabhupada (Teaching of Lord Kapila, Verse 23)*

they can follow-up on – whether it's someone you know, someone who might know someone else, or even a department.

7. **"No, I can't."**

The simplest and most direct way to say no. We build up too many barriers in our mind to saying no. These barriers are self-created and they are not true at all. Don't think so much about saying no and just say it outright. You'll be surprised when the reception isn't half as bad as what you imagined it to be.

*There is story like that. One saintly person was sitting, and some karmis came, that: "You are escaping, you are not working." So he said, "Why shall I work?" "You'll get money." "So what shall I do with the money?" "Then you can live peacefully." "I am living peacefully. Why shall I work?" (laughs) So they want to earn money, keep a good bank balance, and at the end of the life they want to live very peacefully, without any working. But if somebody is living peacefully without working, they will criticize him. They will accuse him, "You are escaping." If the end is this, and I shall live peacefully without any work -- I am doing that in my own standard -- why you are bothering me?*

*~ Srila Prabhupada (Garden Conversation -- June 14, 1976, Detroit)*

# Focused Work

## The Soul of Time Management

Focus Saves Effort And Time

One bright, sunny morning, a large group of young boys gathered by the woodland with their bows and arrows. But these were not just ordinary boys. These were the five Pandavas and hundred Kauravas! The five Pandava brothers and hundred Kaurava brothers were cousins, and a fierce rivalry between them began when they were only children. These young princes would eventually grow into men of incredible power. The five Pandavas were even sons of demigods!

On this day Drona, their mentor and military expert, organized a competition to test their concentration. Across a stream, Drona set up a small wooden bird in a tree. Upon returning to the boys he told them, "Hello children. Today I want to see who among you can strike the eye of that wooden bird across the river."

The bird appeared tiny from where they were standing, but the boys were confident that they could pass their teacher's test. Had they not already felled great beasts on their hunts before? How could this small bird pose such a challenge? Anxiously, each one of the young princes waited for Drona to call their names.

Yudhisthira, the oldest among the Pandavas, was called upon first. Taking position by his teacher, he crouched slightly and drew his bowstring taut.

"Can you see the bird properly? Tell me everything you can see, Yudhisthira," said Drona.

Wanting to be thorough, Yudhisthira began to list off everything that met his eyes. "I see the wooden bird, the branch, and the tree. I can see the leaves moving and even more birds sitting on the same tree. I can see the stream, the grass, other trees, the sky..."

Like this, Yudhisthira named off everything he could think of. When he finished, he waited for his master's final command to shoot. Drona spoke again, "Put down your bow and take a seat Yudhisthira, you will not hit the eye of the bird."

Confused, Yudhisthira silently walked back to his brothers without question. The next boy was called forward and asked the same question by Drona. He gave a similar answer, naming everything he could see. Once again, the the boy was told to put away his bow. This same pattern continued with every boy that followed, until finally Drona reached Arjuna. Drona suppressed a knowing smile as the young prince took his place, notched his bow, and drew his string. Arjuna was one of Drona's favorites.

"Tell me what you can see, Arjuna," repeated Drona.

"I can see only the eye of the bird," replied Arjuna without breaking eye contact with his target.

"Can you not see the trees and the sky? Or perhaps the branch the bird is sitting on?" his mentor asked.

"No sir, all I can see is the eye and nothing else," he said, holding his bow steady and maintaining his unwavering gaze.

Drona was pleased with this response. He cast a glance at the crowd of boys, who were held in silence but slowly began nodding as the lesson began to become clear to them. Drona was happy that one of his favorite pupils was able to pass his test. Now he only had to give the order.

"Shoot!"

With a loud twang, the arrow sprang from the bow straight into the bird's eye. A perfect shot. The bird fell with a small thud as all the boys looked on in amazement at Arjuna.

**FOCUS**
**FOCUS**
**FOCUS**
**FOCUS**
**FOCUS**

After a long pause, Drona patted Arjuna on the back and said, "Now you see, young princes, the power of concentration..."

Bibliography:

"Arjun Home Page." Mantra on Net. Cerebrum Tech, 2005. Web. 1 March 2011. Mantra On Net.

"Arjuna." Wikipedia. Wikipedia, 19 Feb 2011. Web. 1 Mar 2011. Arjuna.

# Improve Your Concentration

## Achieving Focus Amid Distractions

How many times have you sat at your desk and tried to focus on a task, only to find that your mind is wandering? Despite your best intentions, you just can't concentrate. We've all been in this familiar, frustrating situation, and it's something that can really undermine your performance.

Some strategies to improve your concentration and reduce your daily distractions are discussed below.

### Environment

Your personal work environment plays a large role in your ability to concentrate. The more comfortable and welcoming your environment is, the easier it will likely be for you to stay there and focus.

Here are some ideas for improving your physical environment:

I AM FINDING IT DIFFICULT TO CONCENTRATE BUT I AM NOT SURE WHY

**Make sure you're comfortable** – Start by ensuring that your chair and desk are at the right height for you to work comfortably. If your chair is too high or your desk is too low, you'll be uncomfortable, and you'll be tempted to use this as an excuse to get up and walk away.

**Put up pictures** – Viewing a natural scene or watching wildlife can help improve concentration. If you're able to put up pictures in your office or work area, then choose landscapes or natural images that you enjoy. This can help your focus, especially if you can see the pictures from your desk.

**Shut out distractions as much as possible** – Listening to music can help, especially if it's instrumental music. Some people even use noise machines in their offices – these produce a steady "white noise," like ocean waves or falling rain. This steady background noise can drown out other noise, helping you focus better and ignore distractions.

**Nutrition**

Follow some simple nutritional tips:

**Drink water** – Many of us don't think about drinking water while we're at work, yet dehydration can make us feel tired, irritable, slow, or even sick. When our brains don't have enough fluid, they can't operate at peak performance. Staying hydrated is an easy way to help improve your concentration during the day.

The Secret of
Concentration

**Enjoy
What You Do**

Interest ⇌ concentration
(Interest and concentration are proportional to each other)

**Eat breakfast** – Start your day with a healthy breakfast. It's much harder to concentrate when you're hungry, so eat a well-rounded meal before you go to work. You can also help your concentration throughout the day by keeping healthy snacks at your desk. Almonds, whole-grain crackers, fresh fruit, and vegetables are good choices.

**Get up and move around** – Do you walk around during the day? If you're like many people, you probably don't move around enough. Research has shown that regular walking can help increase your focus during the day.

## Mindset

Constant distractions, and the low productivity that's associated with these distractions, have become so commonplace in today's offices that doctors have even given it a name: Attention Deficit Trait, or ADT. And, they say that entire organizations can suffer from it.

Follow some of these guidelines to help focus your mind:

**Set aside time to deal with worries** – Many of us have trouble concentrating during the day because we're constantly worrying about other things. It could be an approaching deadline for a project you haven't started, a new colleague who's causing problems, or just the amount of work on your desk. If you find yourself distracted by worries, then note these down so that you don't need to hold them in your mind. Then schedule time to deal with these issues.

"You arrive early. You work hard. You stay focused. What's your game?"

**Focus on one task at a time** – It can be much harder to focus if you take minibreaks (15–30 seconds) to answer emails, send text messages, or take quick phone calls. Some researchers believe that it can take up to 15 minutes for us to regain complete focus after a distraction.

**Close your email box and chat program** – Let your voice mail do its job. If your office allows it, close your office door or put up a "Do Not Disturb" sign to let colleagues know you need to focus. (If you're a manager and you want to operate an open door policy, then consider working from home or from elsewhere.)

**Switch between high- and low-attention tasks** – This can give your brain a rest after heavy concentration. For instance, if you spend two hours working on your department's budget, you'll probably feel tired afterward. You can recharge your energy by working on a low-attention task, like filing, for 15 minutes before going back to your budget.

**Prioritize** – Having too much to do can be distracting, and this sometime causes procrastination. Or, you may quickly jump from task to task, creating the illusion of work – but in reality, you're not accomplishing very much. If you're not sure which tasks to start or which are most important, take 10 or 15 minutes to prioritize.

### More Tips for Improving Your Concentration

**Take short breaks** – We can be masters at focusing, but eventually we're going to need a break. Our minds can struggle to focus intensely on tasks for eight hours a day. This is where it can be better to divide your work into one-hour segments, with a 5–10 minute

*jihvaikato 'cyuta vikarsati mavitrpta*
*sisno 'nyatas tvag-udaram sravanam kutascit*
*ghrano 'nyatas capala-drk kva ca karma-saktir*
*bahvyah sapatnya iva geha-patim lunanti*

*My dear Lord, O infallible one, my position is like that of a person who has many wives, all trying to attract him in their own way. For example, the tongue is attracted to palatable dishes, the genitals to sex with an attractive woman, and the sense of touch to contact with soft things. The belly, although filled, still wants to eat more, and the ear, not attempting to hear about You, is generally attracted to cinema songs. The sense of smell is attracted to yet another side, the restless eyes are attracted to scenes of sense gratification, and the active senses are attracted elsewhere. In this way I am certainly embarrassed.*

*~ Srimad Bhagavatam (7.9.40)*

break between tasks. This short break will allow your mind to rest before focusing again.

**Do your hardest tasks when you're most alert** – This will help you maximize your concentration. Each of us have our peak energy periods during the day and that's when hardest tasks to be taken up.

**Use a phone headset** – If you have a headset for your phone, consider faking its use for a few hours each day. If your colleagues think you're on the phone, they're less likely to interrupt you.

**Promise yourself a reward** – For instance, make a rule that if you focus intensively for 45 minutes on one task, you can take a break when you're done. Little "self-rewards" can often be great motivators.

**Schedule email downloads** – It can be tremendously distracting to have emails pinging into your inbox every few minutes – you're tempted to stop what you're doing, and answer them right away. If you can, schedule your email to download only a few times each day, and deal with all of your emails in one go.

Reference

Dianna Podmoroff, mindtools

The Art of Concentration: Enhance Focus, Reduce Stress and Achieve More
Harriet Griffey

Concentration: An Approach to Meditation (Quest Books) by Ernest Wood

Scientific Healing Affirmations: Theory and Practice of Concentration by Paramahansa Yogananda

## Use a Planning Tool

Time management experts recommend using a personal planning tool to improve your productivity. Examples of personal planning tools include electronic planners, pocket diaries, calendars, computer programs, wall charts, index cards and notebooks. Writing down your tasks, schedules, and memory joggers can free your mind to focus on your priorities. Auditory learners may prefer to dictate their thoughts instead. The key is to find one planning tool that works for you and use that tool consistently. Some reminders when using a planning tool are:

• Always record your information on the tool itself. Jotting notes elsewhere that have to be transferred later is inefficient.

• Review your planning tool daily.

• Carry your planning tool with you.

• Remember to keep a list of your priorities in your planning tool and refer to it often.

• Synchronize electronic planners with your computer and recharge the batteries in your planner on a regular basis.

• Keep a back-up system.

# Phone Phone Everywhere

How did we get by without our phones before?

The ring of the phone has become almost like Pavlov's bell for some people – we think we must answer it, even if we're concentrating on something important. We let our phones constantly interrupt us. Rings, beeps, chirps. Calls, texts, tweets.

This device allows people to invade your quiet time and insert `their agenda ahead of yours. Phone calls have been a major time bandit ever since the cell phones came, and while they have been joined and probably overtaken by e-mail, they remain a huge drain on human productivity.

"Thank you for calling. Please leave a message. In case I forget to check my messages, please send your message as an audio file to my e-mail, then send me a fax to remind me to check my e-mail, then call back to remind me to check my fax."

### Incoming Calls

**1.** Minimize phone call distractions by turning off your phone during your peak work hours. Or, let your team know that you won't take non-essential calls between specific times, such as from noon to 2 p.m.

**2.** You should never answer the telephone if you don't know who is on the other end. How many times have you answered the phone only to find that you wish you hadn't? Maybe it was somebody trying to sell you something or somebody who you really didn't want to talk to.

When people answer their phone and proceed to tell the caller that they are too busy to talk to him, one of the reasons they are too busy is because they answer their phone and talk to people who are quite simply wasting their time.

**3.** You should never answer calls if you are doing something important. This applies during prime time and quiet time and during meetings.

The whole point of quiet time is that it is time that you have set aside to accomplish something that is important to you on your agenda, and allowing somebody else's agenda to trump yours is a really stupid thing to do.

The usual objection to this is that there are important customers, people you can never reach etc who simply must have instant and unfettered access to you.

Think for a moment about what that attitude says about your relationship with time. There is nothing that is so important that anybody can't wait an hour or so until you get in touch with them.

One of the worst thing you can do is to take telephone calls during meetings. The person who is meeting with you has a substantial prior claim to your time over anybody who simply chooses to call you because it suits their agenda at that time.

**4.** In an office, answer your telephone with a proper business phone greeting. For instance, when answering the phone say something such as, "Cypress Technologies. Madhavi speaking.

How may I help you?" This not only lets the caller know that they've reached a business, but puts the onus on him to answer the question, saving time on exploratory questions such as, "Is this Cypress Technologies?", and idle chit chat.

**5.** Keep a message pad and writing implements by all your phones, so you can jot down details during the inbound phone call.

This is not only good time management at the time, helping to keep you focused on the call, but a help to time management later if you need to find and/or review the details of a particular conversation.

**6.** Give your clients and customers the email option.

Many of them will use email to contact you rather than phoning if they know what your email address is. Ensure that your company's email address is prominent on your business cards and on your website, if you have one.

**7.** Some other steps that you can take to save time in this area:

Use voice mail and set aside time to return calls.

Avoid small talk. Stay focused on the reason for the call.

Stand up while you talk on the phone. You are more likely to keep the conversation brief.

Take any necessary action immediately following the call.

Set aside times of the day for receiving calls and let others know when you are available.

**8.** You Can Turn It Off – Most people don't believe this, but all phones still have an off switch. (Or you can simply put it in Airplane mode). We have been conditioned to be so concerned about "missing" something that we forget this.

### Outgoing Calls

The rules for outbound phone calls are a little simpler. Following is a list of some things that you can do to make yourself more time effective in this area:

**1.** Group the phone calls that you make to be early and late in the day

**2.** Avoid unimportant/routine calls during what you identify as your "prime time".

**3.** Set a goal for every call that you make.

Keep a timer by the phone so that you can keep track of how much time you are really spending.

I WONDER IF SOMEDAY SMART PHONES WILL BE SMARTER THAN US?

WHAT DO YOU MEAN, SOMEDAY?

**4.** Keep something on your desk that you really want to do next so that you have less temptation to stay on the phone and chitchat with the other person and waste your time. If the next thing that you have to do is a "frog" something you really don't want to do, then you'll spend longer on the call.

References

Susan Ward

S Davies, Time Management Edge

Adult Telephone Protocols: Office Version by David A. Thompson

Great Customer Service on the Telephone (Worksmart Series) by Kristin Anderson

# Meetings

### Resolutions, Dissolutions, Revolutions

And No Solutions

There are good meetings and there are bad meetings.

Bad meetings drone on forever, you never seem to get to the point, and you leave wondering why you were even present.

Effective ones leave you energized and feeling that you've really accomplished something.

So what makes a meeting effective?

### Effective Meetings Really Boil Down To Three Things

1. They achieve the meeting's objective.

2. They take up a minimum amount of time.

3. They leave participants feeling that a sensible process has been followed.

If you structure your meeting planning, preparation, execution, and

follow up around these three basic criteria, the result will be an effective meeting.

### 1. The Meeting's Objective

An effective meeting serves a useful purpose. This means that in it, you achieve a desired outcome. For a meeting to meet this outcome, or objective, you have to be clear about what it is.

Too often, people call a meeting to discuss something without really considering what a good outcome would be.

Do you want a decision?

Do you want to generate ideas?

Are you getting status reports?

Are you communicating something?

Are you making plans?

Any of these, and a myriad of others, is an example of a meeting objective. Before you do any meeting planning, you need to focus your objective.

To help you determine what your meeting objective is, complete this sentence:

**At the close of the meeting, I want the group to ...**

With the end result clearly defined, you can then plan the contents of the meeting, and determine who needs to be present.

### 2. Use Time Wisely

With the amount of time we all spend in meetings, you owe it to yourself and your team to streamline the meeting as much as possible. What's more, time wasted in a meeting is time wasted for everybody attending. For example, if a critical person is 15 minutes late in an eight person meeting, that person has cost the organization two hours of lost activity.

Starting with your meeting objective, everything that happens in the meeting itself should further that objective. If it doesn't, it's superfluous and should not be included.

### Agenda

To ensure you cover only what needs to be covered and you stick to relevant activities, you need to create an agenda. The agenda is what you will refer to in order to keep the meeting running on target and on time.

To prepare an agenda, consider the following factors:

Priorities – what absolutely must be covered?

Results – what do need to accomplish at the meeting?

Participants – who needs to attend the meeting for it to be successful?

Sequence – in what order will you cover the topics?

Timing – how much time will spend on each topic?

Date and Time – when will the meeting take place?

Place – where will the meeting take place?

If it's a meeting to solve a problem, ask the participants to come prepared with a viable solution. If you are discussing an ongoing project, have each participant summarize his or her progress to date and circulate the reports amongst members.

Assigning a particular topic of discussion to various people is another great way to increase involvement and interest. On the agenda, indicate who will lead the discussion or presentation of each item.

**Use your agenda as your time guide.** When you notice that time is running out for a particular item, consider hurrying the discussion, pushing to a decision, deferring discussion until another time, or assigning it for discussion by a subcommittee.

### 3. Satisfying Participants that a Sensible Process Has Been Followed

Once you have an agenda prepared, you need to circulate it to the participants and get their feedback and input. Running a meeting is not a dictatorial role: You have to be participative right from the start.

Perhaps there is something important that a team member has to add. Maybe you have allotted too much, or too little, time for a particular item. There may even be some points you've included that have been settled already and can be taken off the list for discussion.

Whatever the reason, it is important you get feedback from the meeting participants about your proposed agenda.

Once in the meeting, to ensure maximum satisfaction for everyone, there are several things you should keep in mind:

If certain people are dominating the conversation, make a point of asking others for their ideas.

At the end of each agenda item, quickly summarize what was said, and ask people to confirm that that's a fair summary. Then make notes regarding follow-up.

You need to stop someone from speaking too much. Ensure the meeting stays on topic.

List all tasks that are generated at the meeting. Make a note of who is assigned to do what, and by when.

*"Before we discuss destroying the competition, screwing our customers, and laughing all the way to the bank, let's begin this meeting with a prayer."*

At the close of the meeting, quickly summarize next steps and inform everyone that you will be sending out a meeting summary.

After the meeting is over, take some time to debrief, and determine what went well and what could have been done better. Evaluate the meeting's effectiveness based on how well you met the objective. This will help you continue to improve your process of running effective meetings.

Finally, prepare the meeting summary. This will be forwarded to all participants and other stakeholders. It is a record of what was accomplished and who is responsible for what as the team moves forward.

This is a very crucial part of effective meetings that often gets overlooked. You need a written record of what transpired, along with a list of actions that named individuals have agreed to perform. Make sure someone is assigned to take notes during the meeting.

Reference

Tom Hallett, Mindtools

Douglass, M. 1998. Time Management

101: Secrets for Succeeding in a Busy World. Tulsa, OK: Advantage Quest Publ.

## Email Management

While email is incredibly useful, it's also one of the biggest work distractions we face. Many of us could spend entire days simply reading and responding to emails.

Researchers encourage people to try to limit their usage of email dialogue boxes, sound alerts, and the frequency that they are updated about new emails.

Some steps are suggested to tackle the email menace:

1. Employees in a workplace are discouraged from using the reply-to-all feature to prevent unnecessary distractions to peers who will find not find the email useful.

2. Schedule "email" times – Minimize this distraction by scheduling specific times to check and respond to emails. For instance, you could check email when you first arrive at work, at lunch, and right before you leave, and specify a half-hour slot every day to respond to your emails. (If you do this, it may

8 DAYS AND 26 EMAILS TO ACHIEVE WHAT COULD'VE BEEN DONE IN A 1 MINUTE CONVERSATION.

be useful to let co-workers and customers know that they will need to contact you another way if they need you urgently.)

3. Check and respond to email at "low productivity" times – Remember that there are certain times of day when you probably do your best work. Some people work best in the morning, and others late at night. Schedule your email check-in during your less-productive times – and save your peak hours for doing creative, high-value work.

4. Keep your email program closed – When you're not using your email program, close it entirely – or at least turn off the visual or audible alerts that distract you. This eliminates the temptation to check it constantly.

5. It helps to set your email software to "receive" messages only at certain times, so that you're not distracted by incoming messages. If you can't do this, at least make sure that you turn off audible and visual alerts.

### Two-Minute Rule

Try using the "Two-Minute Rule" (a concept from David Allen, the author of Getting Things Done ) when you read your mail – if the email will take less than two minutes to read and reply to, then take care of it right now, even if it's not a high priority. The idea behind this is that if it takes less than two minutes to action, it would take longer to store the task away .

For emails that will take longer than two minutes to read or respond to, schedule time on your calendar, or add this as an action on your To-Do List , to do later. Most email programs allow you to highlight, flag, or star messages that need a response, so utilize this handy feature whenever you can.

### FYI Emails

Many of us also get lots of internal notifications. These are those "FYI" emails from the corporate office or from team members who want to keep us "in the loop." If you see your name in the "cc" field instead of the "To" field, chances are it's an FYI email. Consider filing it in a "To Read" folder, and tackle it when you have time.

Filing System

Set up a simple filing system to help manage your mail.

You could use broad categories titled "Action Items," "Waiting," "Reference," and "Archives." If you're able to stay on top of your folders – particularly "Action" and "Waiting" folders – you could use them as an informal To-Do List for the day.

If four categories sounds too simplistic for your needs, you can set up a more detailed system. For instance, you could create a folder for every project that you're working on, or have a set folder for each of your clients or sales reps.

The advantage when you create specific folders for processing email is that it makes it easier to search for past mail: instead of scouring your entire email system, you can simply search in that particular folder.

## Using Rules

Most email programs, such as Outlook and Gmail, allow you to establish "Rules" that sort email into a particular folder as soon as it comes in.

For instance, you might get several emails per day that notify you of sales that your company has made. You want to receive these, because you want to see what's happening, but you don't want them to clutter your inbox.

This is where you could set up a rule in your email program that moves emails with, say, "Sale Notification:" in the subject line straight to the "Sales Made" folder as soon as they come in. This means that you don't need to manually file these emails, and allows you to keep all of the sales emails in one folder.

### Non-Essential Email

If you regularly receive email such as newsletters, blogs and article feeds, you could re-route these to another email address, or use rules, so that they're instantly delivered to a particular folder.

This will help keep your primary inbox clear, and they'll be in one place, ready to read at a convenient time.

### Precision

You can make a world of difference for your colleagues, boss, and clients when you write effective emails . This will not only save them stress and frustration, but succinct, relevant emails can also save an enormous amount of time – yours and theirs.

Even though he used it every day, Harry never understood where e-mail came from.

### Good Team Habits

One of the best things that you can do, to limit the amount of email you need to process, is encourage people to send you less.

For instance, if certain team members regularly send you long, drawn-out emails, let them know. Tell them gently but firmly that because of the demand on your time, you'd appreciate emails no longer than a paragraph or two. Anything longer than that should warrant a phone call. Alternatively, they could drop by your office for a discussion.

References

Andrews P. (2004) Vying for your attention: Interruption management, Executive Technology Report

Gillie T. & Broadbent D. (1989) What makes interruptions disruptive? A study of length, similarity and complexity, Psychological Research, 50 (4), 243-250

Carroll, John M. "Notification and awareness: synchronizing task-oriented collaborative activity". International Journal of Human-Computer Studies.

## Until The Sun Set

**Treasure Is All Yours**

Once, a king and a lazy man were good friends, having studied together in childhood. One morning, the king enquired, "You appear to be quite poor. Why don't you work to earn some money?"

The lazy man said, "No one gives me a job. My critics have informed everyone that I never do any work on time."

The kind king said, "Today, you can go into my treasury and collect as much wealth as you can, till sunset."

The lazy man rushed home to inform his wife. She exclaimed, "Hurry up! Get as much wealth as you can."

"But I am too hungry right now. Let me have a quick lunch."

Joyfully he had lunch, feeling elated by the developments. After lunch, he set out for the palace. As he walked in the searing heat, he

sat under a tree to relax. As he sat under the tree's cooling shade, he dozed off and 2 hours passed by. He got up and rushed to the palace.

As he was nearing the palace, he saw a juggler showing tricks. He halted to watch and after sometime realized it's getting late. He ran but by the time the Sun had set and palace gates had been shut.

The lazy man remained poor as before.

Many of us are that lazy man. Every morning The King called Time throws open his treasury of 86,400 golden seconds. They are ours to collect. As much as we can. As soon as the day is over, the palace doors are shut and the opportunity is lost. Those who are intelligent, they gather as much of these golden moments as they can and become time rich. Others, distracted by temporary enjoyment, rot in perpetual poverty. Choice is entirely left to an individual.

*ayur harati vai pumsam*
*udyann astam ca yann asau*
*tasyarte yat-ksano nita*
*uttama-sloka-vartaya*
*Both by rising and by setting, the sun decreases the duration of life of everyone, except one who utilizes the time by discussing topics of the all-good Personality of Godhead.*
*~Srimad Bhagavatam 2.3.17*

# The Curse of Commuting

Work Closer To Home Or Go Back To Rural Life of Self Sufficiency

No matter who you are, you have a story to tell about the dreaded daily commute. According to the Research and Innovative Technology Administration (RITA), in 2008, 96% of the 144 million workers in the US commute to work on a full or part-time basis. 76% of those workers drive alone, 11% carpool with others, and only 5% use public transportation. Keep in mind that the average number of miles driven to work (one way) increased by 42% from 1983 to 2001 to an average of 12 miles, and it's easy to see how our dreaded commute is only going to get more dreadful as the years go on.

In fact, a 2007 study done by BusinessWeek Research Services and TransitCenter in three major metropolitan areas (Chicago, New York, and San Francisco) showed that 80% of commuters are concerned with the cost of commuting. 92% with the high cost of fuel, and 48% thought their commute was getting worse. Overall, more than a quarter of commuters would potentially take another job due to commuting difficulties.

Ignoring the strain of commuting on our workforce won't do us any favours. Eventually, the stress adds up and taunts even our top talent with "finding a job closer to home".

The average travel time to work is 25 minutes, equivalent to two work weeks each years (or what an average employee takes in vacation time) – and that's only one way; the return trip is just as long, according to the U.S. Census Bureau's 2008 American Community Survey.

By comparison, the European Union residents fare even worse with an average commute time of 38 minutes, according to the Royal Automobile Club in the United Kingdom. The majority of motorists surveyed in 20 cities on six continents say that traffic has worsened in the past three years. And spare a thought for "extreme commuters", the US Census Bureau moniker for Americans who spend more than 90 minutes each way. Since 1990, their number has nearly doubled to 3.5 million, a 95% increase since 1990.

Similarly, roadway congestion accounts for a significant portion of the time and cost of commuting. In the US, from a survey of 439 US urban areas, the proportion of time spent in travel delays increased from 10% to 29% between 1982 and 2007. This congestion is doing an insurmountable toll on our environment. The annual cost of wasted time and fuel add up to 36 hours and 24 gallons, almost the same as a full work week and a quarter tonne of extra $CO_2$.

This is not to downplay the heavy psychological toll commuting takes on our workforce as well. A 2004 study of commuters found extreme stress levels on part with fighter pilots going into battle or riot policemen on the front line. In fact, a 2004 paper based on 14 years of research on German commuters found that, contrary to what economics would normally predict, the benefits of commuting, such as a higher income and lower housing costs, do not fully compensate the burden of commuting. People who have longer commutes were systematically worse off, left with a lower subjective well-being.

Finally, as you will have guessed, commuting also has a direct cost to employers. In a 2009 study, traffic was the most reported reason for being late, cited 33% of the time. As lateness eats into company time, many early morning activities and meetings can be delayed or rescheduled entirely, which becomes a hassle when working with employees who work different hours.

Commuting has direct negative effects for both employers and employees, so who benefits from it? If the answer is no one, perhaps it's time to rethink the way we define commuting.

References:

Global Workplace Analytics

The Freedom To Work, March 1, 2014

The Research and Innovative Technology Administration (RITA)

BusinessWeek Research Services and TransitCenter, The Impact of Commuting On Employees, 2008.

U.S. Census Bureau, 2008 American Community Survey.

Business Week, February 21, 2005: Extreme Commuting.

Texas Transportation Institute, 2009 Urban Mobility Report.

*Contemporary civilization is by in large an assembly of animals because, as stated before, it operates on the basis of the animal propensities. The birds and beasts arise early in the morning and busy themselves trying to find food and sex and trying to defend themselves; at night they look for shelter, and in the morning they fly to a tree to find nuts and fruits. Similarly, in New York City, great hordes of people travel from one island to another by ferry boat or wait for subways in order to go to the office for the purpose of finding food. How is this an advancement over animal life? Although the ferry and subway are always crowded, and many people have to travel forty or fifty miles for bread, the birds are free to fly from one tree to another.*

*Real civilization is not concerned simply with man's animal needs but with enabling man to understand his relationship with God, the supreme father.*

*~ Srila Prabhupada (Matchless Gifts 6: Transcending Designations and Problems)*

# Paper Management

## Organizing Ideas For All That Paper!

Why do we let paper collect in piles around us? Is it because we're afraid of paper? Is there an epidemic of Papyrophobia? Nah, we just have lots of little, but real fears.

Do you waste your time looking for important information kept on an elusive piece of paper, do you feel out of control when you can't find that piece of paper? Here's the answer to your questions and the cure for your fears, Paper Management! Managing paper is no mystery; it just takes time to set up the system initially and then all you have to do is maintain it.

There is nothing new or complex about the age old adage, "a place for everything and everything in it's place." Instead of assigning many places for your paper, assign it to ONE place, your computer. Go Paperless by digitizing all things paper and you'll never have to scramble for it again!

One of the key tools you need is a paper scanner along with intuitive software. Many scanners automatically detect Documents, Business Cards and Receipts and then accurately categorize them for you. You can create a file system within the software program to mirror your paper file system. In the meantime, you have a virtually paperless space. The obvious papers you keep, for example your birth certificate and other important papers can still be digitized and kept compactly in a smaller space. You won't waste time looking for papers, you will be in control of your space and you'll have peace of mind.

Here's a few books that could help you get on track with Paper Management:

1. Taming the Paper Tiger by Barbra Hemphill

2. Getting Things Done: The Art of Stress Free Productivity by David Allen

3. Organizing from the Inside Out by Julie Morgenstern

Take the time and be good to yourself as you work towards your Paper Management goals!

Reference:

Paper Management with Sarah Sain, October 30th, 2012

Anderson, Chris. Is Document Control Really That Important?

# Frivolous Sports

## Squandering Away Time And Money

S ports have always existed in human society but never at the present day scale. In our culture today, too much time is spent watching sports on TV, following one's favorite team, playing fantasy football, and debating over players' merits.

Many sports fans would attest to the time they have wasted that could have been otherwise spent in learning an instrument, reading a book, meeting new people, or engaging in some other intellectual activity.

Sports like foot ball, hockey are played for a shorter duration, but cricket can waste your whole day or even continuous 5 days. Then you waste more days discussing it with your friends.

"Baseball is not our national pastime.
Baseball scandals are our national pastime."

Lot of these games are fixed by the players for money. International betting rackets are actively involved in match fixing. Players make money while making a mockery of millions of viewers who are wasting their valuable time.

Sports just celebrate the animal faculties in human beings such as the ability to jump and run, but nothing which distinguishes humans from animals and makes humans noble, such as philosophy, poetry and music. They might as well have Olympic medals for vomiting and diarrhea one day, which are also crude activities we share with animals.

In last 10 years, over 120 billion dollars have been spent on games. That includes Olympics, winter Olympics, football world cups, commonwealth games etc.

The Chinese Olympics was the most expensive sports event in human history, entailing a budget of over $48 billion. In the recently concluded winter Olympics in Sochi, Russia, $30 billion were spent. And the Olympic city is falling apart already. The only residents left are the stray dogs. India also spent billions in organizing commonwealth games, marred by shameless scandals, while boasting the largest population of malnourished children in the world.

And all this to check out who can run faster, who can jump higher, who can swim better and who can punch harder. But animals all around us can accomplish this much better, without spending billions and without any gorgeous arrangements.

"I don't get it. If they all want the ball so badly, why don't they just buy more balls?!"

And these billions can solve ALL the world problems if spent wisely. Out of Beijing Olympic's 48 billion dollars, 40 billion dollars would have sufficed, according to UNHDR, to achieve universal access to basic social services in ALL developing countries:

| Global Priority | $U.S. Billions |
|---|---|
| Basic education for all | 6 |
| Water and sanitation for all | 9 |
| Reproductive health for all women | 12 |
| Basic health and nutrition | 13 |

(Source: The state of human development, United Nations Human Development Report 1998, Chapter 1, p.37)

Therefore mismanagement of the world resources in the real cause of all our problems. We are squandering away our time and money shamelessly.

> The class friends wanted to play in the tiffin hour and Prahlada Maharaja asked them to sit down and to learn God consciousness. So the class friend protested, "My dear friend, why you are insisting now? We are now children, let us play." That Prahlada Maharaja protested, "No, no, you should not waste your time playing because this God consciousness should be learned from the very beginning of life." Kaumara acaret prajno dharman bhagavatan iha [SB 7.6.1]. From the very childhood Krsna consciousness should be learned. Why from the, so early, that durlabham manusam janma tad apy adhruvam arthadam. He says that this human form of life you have got after many, many millions of births so we should not misuse this opportunity. We do not know when we shall meet next death, but if before meeting the next death we make our life perfect in Krsna consciousness that is the special boon to this human form of life. We should utilize it.
> ~ Srila Prabhupada (Philosophy Discussions, John Stuart Mill)

## ABC analysis

A technique that has been used in business management for a long time is the categorization of large data into groups. These groups are often marked A, B, and C—hence the name. Activities are ranked by these general criteria:

A – Tasks that are perceived as being urgent and important,

B – Tasks that are important but not urgent,

C – Tasks that are neither urgent nor important. (This list could also include tasks that are urgent but not important.)

Each group is then rank-ordered by priority. To further refine the prioritization, some individuals choose to then force-rank all "B" items as either "A" or "C". ABC analysis can incorporate more than three groups.

ABC analysis is frequently combined with Pareto analysis.

An early advocate of "ABC" prioritization was Alan Lakein, in 1973. In his system "A" items were the most important ("A-1" the most important within that group), "B" next most important, "C" least important.

A particular method of applying the ABC method assigns "A" to tasks to be done within a day, "B" a week, and "C" a month.

To prioritize a daily task list, one either records the tasks in the order of highest priority, or assigns them a number after they are listed ("1" for highest priority, "2" for second highest priority, etc.) which indicates in which order to execute the tasks. The latter method is generally faster, allowing the tasks to be recorded more quickly.

Another way of prioritizing compulsory tasks (group A) is to put the most unpleasant one first. When it's done, the rest of the list feels easier. Groups B and C can benefit from the same idea, but instead of doing the first task (which is the most unpleasant) right away, it gives motivation to do other tasks from the list to avoid the first one.

Reference:

Practice the ABC Method - Brian Tracy

Emerald Insight | Multiple Criteria ABC Analysis

Tom Hallett, The ABC Technique - Stress Management From MindTools

## Pareto Analysis

The pareto principle, also known as the law of the vital few or the 80/20 principle, states that 20% of something will cause 80% of the results. This implies that 20% of your effort, would complete 80% of a project. The rule is also applicable to almost all areas of life: economy, sport, earnings, clients, problems, health, software... You can go on and on. The real question is, how do you use it to your advantage

In time management it implies that 80% of tasks can be completed in 20% of the disposable time. The remaining 20% of tasks will take up 80% of the time. This principle is used to sort tasks into two parts. According to this form of Pareto analysis it is

recommended that tasks that fall into the first category be assigned a higher priority.

The 80-20-rule can also be applied to increase productivity: it is assumed that 80% of the productivity can be achieved by doing 20% of the tasks. Similarly, 80% of results can be attributed to 20% of activity. If productivity is the aim of time management, then these tasks should be prioritized higher. This view of the Pareto Principle is explored further in The 4-Hour Workweek by Timothy Ferriss.

It depends on the method adopted to complete the task. There is always a simpler and easier way to complete the task. If one uses a complex way, it will be time consuming. So, one should always try to find out the alternate ways to complete each task.

Reference:

Lakein, Alan (1973). How to Get Control of Your Time and Your Life. New York: P.H. Wyden. ISBN 0-451-13430-3.

"14-Day Action Challenge". 14-Day Action Challenge.

The 4-Hour Workweek, Timothy Ferris, Crown Publishing Group 2007

## POSEC Method

POSEC is an acronym for Prioritize by Organizing, Streamlining, Economizing and Contributing. The method dictates a template which emphasizes an average individual's immediate sense of emotional and monetary security. It suggests that by attending to one's personal responsibilities first, an individual is better positioned to shoulder collective responsibilities.

Inherent in the acronym is a hierarchy of self-realization, which mirrors Abraham Maslow's hierarchy of needs:

Prioritize - Your time and define your life by goals.

Organize - Things you have to accomplish regularly to be successful (Family and Finances).

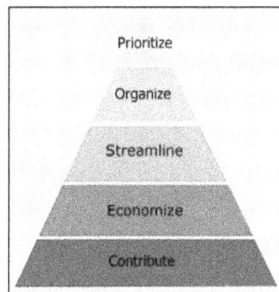

Streamline - Things you may not like to do, but must do (Work and Chores).

Economize - Things you should do or may even like to do, but they're not pressingly urgent (Pastimes and Socializing).

Contribute - By paying attention to the few remaining things that make a difference (Social Obligations).

April 22

# Aim To "Eat An Elephant Beetle"

**First Thing, Every Day!**

Eating an Elephant Beetle at the start of your workday is the best way to ensure that you will not have to tackle anything worse that day.

You know what your Elephant Beetle is, it's that task that you keep putting off – the one that haunts you and sits on your shoulder all day long, reminding you that it needs to get done no matter how much you don't want to do it.

If you make it your priority to get it done first thing, the sense of relief at having gotten rid of the burden will carry you through the rest of the Day regardless of what else is thrown at you. Productivity breeds productivity, and the self-satisfaction you get from it can't be beat.

Start everyday by completing that task that you know you have to, but just don't want to. After that, everything else you do will seem so easy in comparison.

The book by Brian Tracy, Eat That Frog also deals with the same topic. It also recommends to focus on tasks that we don't like and keep putting off.

## Nightly Planning

This is simple. Before you go to sleep, plan out the following day. It's easier to stay focused when you've already mapped out the day in your mind.

According to Dr. Donald E. Wetmore, you've wound down from the workday and are less pressured at night. The major benefit, however, it that by having a plan of action completed the night before, you go to bed with a sense of certainty and control about your next day and with a sense of anticipation you would not ordinarily have.

After getting into the habit of accomplishing your Daily Planning each night, the quality of your sleep will be enhanced because you have established a plan each night that gives you the roadmap or game plan for the next day eliminating the need to wrestle with all the loose ends in your heads during our sleeping hours, interfering with the quality of your sleep.

Put the plan into writing. There is extraordinary power in the pen. Putting your plan into writing helps us to increase your feelings of control and, indeed, the reality of control. When you try to keep track of everything in your heads, things tend to slip through the cracks.

# Power of Pen

## And Paper

### And Making A List

Charles Schwab, President of Bethlehem Steel, and the same name you know today as one of the leading investment houses, paid Ivy Lee $25,000 for this time management techniques benefits over 100 years ago. If it was worth so much to Schwab, don't you think its worth learning too?

Around 100 years ago, Charles Schwab, president of Bethlehem Steel, wanted to increase his own efficiency, and of the management team at the steel company. Ivy Lee, a well-known efficiency expert of the time, approached Mr. Schwab, and made a proposition Charles Schwab could not refuse:

Ivy Lee: "I can increase your people's efficiency – and your sales – if you will allow me to spend fifteen minutes with each of your executives."

Charles Schwab: "How much will it cost me?"

Ivy Lee: "Nothing, unless it works. After three months, you can send me a check for whatever you feel it's worth to you."

Charles Schwab: "It's a deal."

The following day, Ivy Lee met with Charles Schwab's management executives, spending only ten minutes with each in order to tell them:

Ivy Lee: "I want you to promise me that for the next ninety days, before leaving your office at the end of the day, you will make a list of the six most important things you have to do the next day and number them in their order of importance."

Astonished Executives: "That's it?"

Ivy Lee: "That's it. Scratch off each item after finishing it, and go on to the next one on your list. If something doesn't get done, put it on the following day's list."

"Each Bethlehem executive consented to follow Lee's instructions. Three months later, Schwab studied the results and was so pleased that he sent Lee a check for $25,000.

If Schwab, one of the smartest businessmen of his day, was willing to pay so much money for this advice, don't you think you could benefit from it too?

Taking advantage of this time management technique is as simple as it gets…just 4 steps:

1. At the end of each day, make a list of the top 6 things you want to accomplish the following day

2. Prioritize the list

3. Start working on task number one, and keep working on it until you complete it. Do not move onto the next task until you complete this one.

4. If any tasks are left at the end of the day, move them to the top of the next days list. For example, if you finish tasks 1-4 today, tasks 5 and 6 become tasks 1 and 2 on tomorrows list.

# Energizing Yourself

## Powering Through Your Day

A glass of water can help you to regain your energy.
Imagine that it's 2:30 p.m., and that you've run into a brick wall at work.

You can barely keep your eyes open, and you're struggling to stay focused.

All you want to do is take a nap.

At times like this, you may make poor decisions or feel irritable, or you may struggle to deliver high-quality work or meet deadlines. And you may lack the energy to push ahead with new initiatives.

Let's face it: to do our best, we need to be energized throughout the day!

In this article, we'll look at what lies behind low energy levels, and we'll explore what you can do to boost them.

### What Causes Low Energy?

There are many reasons why your energy levels may be low. For example, this could be caused by:

- Lack of sleep.
- Poor diet.
- Iron or vitamin deficiencies.

- Medication.
- Lack of exercise.
- Depression.
- Burnout or stress.
- Underactive thyroid.
- Low motivation.

Fatigue may be a symptom of a physical or mental health problem. You might need medical attention.

### Short-Term Solutions

Give yourself a quick boost in any of these ways.

### Rehydrate Yourself

Our bodies need water to function. When you're dehydrated, you're depriving yourself of vital fuel, and this can affect your memory as well as your energy levels.

As soon as you feel your energy flagging, reach for a tall glass of water. The Institute of Medicine suggests that men should drink around 3 liters of fluid over the course of a day, and that women drink around 2.2 liters.

This fluid need not be water. However, if you choose another drink, be aware that its ingredients may offset the benefits of pure water. For example, caffeine can cause anxiety, while high-sugar drinks may give a short-term energy boost that's followed by deeper fatigue.

Drink plenty of water during and after exercise to replenish fluid levels.

### Use Light

If your office has a window, open the blinds to let in plenty of natural light.

If you don't have access to a window, make sure that your lamps are bright enough. Lamps that emit the full spectrum of light (similar to sunlight) can make you feel more alert.

Even the light emitted by your monitor can have an impact, as increased light can suppress sleep-inducing hormones. Adjust the brightness settings on your screen to increase the amount of light given out.

You may also find that a daylight lamp boosts your energy levels. These lamps, designed for people experiencing seasonal affective disorder, are also thought to improve mental alertness.

### Take a Walk

A short walk will increase the flow of oxygen to your brain.

You may also find that a change of surroundings, even for a short time, increases your energy levels. If you can, walk with a friend or colleague; this may encourage you to walk further, and can also boost your self-esteem.

Aim to walk in surroundings with good light to take advantage of the added effects that light has on energy levels.

### Music

Think about how you feel when you listen to an upbeat, high-energy track. Your attention sharpens, you start tapping your feet, and your spirits seem to rise.

Music can have a profound effect on energy levels. Certain types of music can make you feel more energized, attentive, and awake, while other styles can make you feel calm, sleepy, angry, or tense. The type of music most likely to raise your energy level is highly

*Yes, everything requires little enthusiasm. Just like a boy is going to school with no enthusiasm, and a boy is going to school with nice enthusiasm. One boy is passing in the first class, first division and another boy is failing or he's passing in the third division.*
*~ Srila Prabhupada (Interview -- March 9, 1968, San Francisco)*

personal. You may find that classical music or jazz restores your energy, while others prefer something else.

Music can be energizing, but it can also be distracting. Think about your tasks and whether listening to music could affect your ability to complete them well.

For example, many people find that they cannot concentrate on fine detail when they're listening to music with lyrics. Use well-fitting headphones to avoid spreading your sound.

### Other Techniques

Depending on the culture of your workplace, you could try other short-term energy-boosting techniques.

For example, aromatherapy - using scents to address specific ailments or conditions - has been shown to be effective at combating fatigue. One study found that the scent of lime made participants feel more alert than those in the control group.

Your colleagues may not welcome aromatherapy in the office, however. The essential oils used can cause sensitivities, and some oils should not be used near people with diabetes, or near pregnant or nursing women.

### Short Nap

A short nap can also help you feel more alert. However, your organization may not approve of you "sleeping on the job."

If you're considering this, talk to your boss about whether a short afternoon nap (20 minutes or less) would be appropriate in your workplace. Ask how he or she feels about you taking a short break to nap, even if it's in your car.

## Long-Term Solutions

There are plenty of long-term strategies for improving your energy and focus at work, too.

### Eat Healthier Food

Your diet has a huge effect on how you feel. When you eat poor-quality foods (such as those high in fat, sugar, salt, and artificial ingredients), you don't take in the nutrients that you need to perform at your best.

Some of these foods, such as candy bars or chips, do provide a quick burst of energy by raising your blood sugar levels. However, those levels quickly drop, often leaving you feeling even worse than you did beforehand.

Instead of eating salty or sugary snacks, aim to eat three well-balanced meals every day. You may also want to eat healthy mid-morning and mid-afternoon snacks. These include walnuts or almonds, low-fat cheese and whole-grain crackers, fruits and vegetables and yogurt.

### Exercise Regularly

One of the best ways to boost your energy is to get regular exercise. Countless studies suggest that exercise is an essential part of a healthy lifestyle.

*A Krsna conscious person never tires of working, and the symptoms I can see in you as you want to be overloaded with work. This is the test of how one is advancing in Krsna consciousness. Nobody becomes more tired but wants to work more and more. Your Godbrother Satsvarupa told me the same thing that he may be overloaded with typewriting work. Similarly, Govinda dasi and Gaurasundara also want to be overloaded with work. So your examples are great encouragement for an old man like me. I have got the same spirit of being overloaded with Krsna conscious work, but physically I am not as strong as you are all young boys and girls."*
*(SPL to Jadurani, 16th December, 1967)*

Regular exercise has also been shown to increase memory and a sense of well-being.

No matter how busy you are, try to make exercise part of your daily routine.

### Find Meaning

Sometimes your energy can wane when you're working on a task that you find boring or meaningless. Routine tasks can numb your mind, and make you feel tired or lethargic.

Look at the tasks that seem to sap your energy the most. These "energy vampires" are often the urgent but not important tasks that you must do regularly. Use theUrgent/Important Matrix to see how much time you're devoting to these tasks.

Ask yourself whether you really need to accomplish these tasks; if not, see if you can cancel them, or delegate them to someone who may find them more satisfying.

If you've lost some of your enthusiasm for your role, re-examine the purpose in what you do.

### Look At Your Schedule

How you schedule tasks can also affect your energy. For example, if you're a "morning person," you'll have the most energy before lunch. Your energy might drop in the afternoon and then pick up again in the early evening. If this is the case for you, schedule your hardest, most important tasks in the morning, during your peak energy time.

> *Of course, it is not pride, but take from example of my life. I was retired in Vrndavana, and at seventy years old I thought that it was to be done: "Nobody did it. Let me try." So I came to America. Today is the tenth anniversary. (devotees cheer) So at least from material calculation, if I had not taken that risk... When I was coming, my friends and others said, "This man is going to die." "Never mind," I thought, "death will come. Let me try." So this enthusiasm must be there.*
>
> *~ Srila Prabhupada (Sri Caitanya-caritamrta, Madhya-lila 20.101 -- Washington, D.C., July 6, 1976)*

April 26

# Leverage

## Achieving Much More with the Same Effort

G ive me a lever long enough and a place to stand, and I can move the Earth."– Archimedes

To lift a heavy object, you have a choice: use leverage or not. You can try to lift the object directly – risking injury – or you can use a lever, such as a jack or a long plank of wood, to transfer some of the weight, and then lift the object that way.

Which approach is wiser? Will you succeed without using leverage? Maybe. But you can lift so much more with leverage, and do it so much more easily!

So what has this got to do with your life and career?

The answer is "a lot". By applying the concept of leverage to business and career success, you can, with a little thought, accomplish very much more than you can without it. Without leverage, you may work very hard, but your rewards are limited by the hours you put in. With leverage, you can break this connection and, in time, achieve very much more.

We're not referring to financial leverage here. Financial leverage, using "other people's money" to grow your business, can be a successful growth strategy. However, it's outside the scope of this article.

### Levers of Success

So how can you apply leverage to your life? And how can you achieve much more, while-if you choose to-reducing the number of hours that you work?

To do this, you'll need to learn how to use the leverage of:-

- Time (yours and that of other people).
- Resources.
- Knowledge and education.
- Technology.

### Time Leverage

Using the leverage of time is the most fundamental strategy for success. There are only so many hours in a day that you can work. If you use only your own time, you can achieve only so much. If you leverage other people's time, you can increase productivity to an extraordinary extent.

**To Leverage Your Own Time.**

- Practice effective time management. Eliminate unnecessary activities, and focus your effort on the things that really matter.
- As part of this, learn how to prioritize, so that you focus your energy on the activities that give the greatest return for the time invested.

- Use goal setting to think about what matters to you in the long term, set clear targets, and motivate yourself to achieve those targets.

**To Leverage Other People's Time.**

- Learn how to delegate work to other people.
- Train and empower others (through team building).

• Bring in experts and consultants to cover skill or knowledge gaps.

• Outsource non-core tasks to people with the experience to do them more efficiently.

Providing that you do things properly, the time and money that you invest in leveraging other people's time is usually well spent.

This is why delegation is such an important skill: If you can't delegate effectively, you can never expand your productivity beyond the work that you can personally deliver. This means that your career will quickly stall, and while you may be appreciated for your hard work, you'll never be truly successful.

It's also one of the reasons that micromanagement is such a vice: You spend so much time managing a few people that you constrain the amount of leverage you can exert.

## Resource Leverage

You can also exert leverage by getting the most from your assets, and taking full advantage of your personal strengths.

You have a wide range of skills, talents, experiences, thoughts, and ideas. These can, and should, be used in the best combination. What relevant skills and strengths do you have that others don't? How can you use these to best effect, and how can you improve them so that they're truly remarkable? What relevant assets do you have that others don't? Can you use these to create leverage? Do you have connections that others don't have? Or financial resources? Or some other asset that you can use to greater effect?

A good way of thinking about this is to conduct a personal SWOT analysis, focusing on identifying strengths and assets, and expanding from these to identify the opportunities they give you.

(An advantage of SWOT is that it also helps you spot critical weaknesses that need to be covered.)

### Knowledge and Education Leverage

Another significant lever of success is applied knowledge. Combined with education and action, this can generate tremendous leverage.

Learning by experience is slow and painful. If you can find more formal ways of learning, you'll progress much more quickly. What's more, if you select a good course, you'll have a solid foundation to your knowledge, and one that doesn't have high-risk gaps. This is why people working in life-or-death areas (such as architects, airline pilots, medical doctors and suchlike) need long and thorough training. After all, would you want to be operated on by an unqualified surgeon?

The keys to successfully leveraging knowledge and education are: firstly, knowing what you need to learn; secondly knowing to what level you need to learn it; thirdly, being very focused and selective in your choices; and fourthly, in taking the time to earn the qualifications you need.

Even then, having more education or more knowledge isn't necessarily a point of leverage. These become advantages only when they can be directly applied to your career goals and aspirations--and when they're used actively and intelligently to do something useful.

By hiring, consulting with, and outsourcing to other people, you gain the leverage of their knowledge and education as well as their resources. This only works if you choose the right people – the wrong ones can slow you and drag you down. Don't let this happen!

### Technology Leverage

Finding technology leverage is all about thinking about how you work, and using technology to automate as much of this as you can.

At a simple level, you might find that all you need to keep you in touch with home and work is a laptop computer. Alternatively, a personal digital assistant (PDA) can help you maintain a single, convenient, properly-backed-up time management system. Cell phones that access email and browse the web are handy tools for making the best of your downtime during working hours or while traveling. If you're a slow typist, voice recognition software can help you dictate documents and save time.

At a more sophisticated level, you may find that you can use simple desktop databases like Microsoft Access to automate simple work processes. If you do a lot of routine data processing (for example, if you run many similar projects) you can find that this saves you a great deal of time. More than this, you only need to set up a process once with a tool like this – afterwards the process will be executed the same way each time, by whomever initiates the process (this reduces training, meaning that new team members can become productive much more quickly, meaning that you can scale your operations-and your success-more quickly.)

Businesses can choose from a wide array of software solutions. Some of these can automate or simplify tasks that are otherwise very time-consuming. Customer relationship management (CRM) databases can bring tremendous benefits for sales and customer service organizations, as can point-of-sale (PoS) inventory systems for organizations that need to track and manage inventory. Websites and web-based catalogs can give clients easy access to up-to-date product information, and help them place orders simply and easily. And blogs and email-based newsletters help people stay in contact with thousands of people quickly and easily. All of these use technology to provide tremendous leverage.

To conclude, surround yourself with a network of great people who have skills, knowledge, and expertise that you don't possess. Look for opportunities to create synergy, and leverage the talents of everyone involved. When you work together, you can accomplish so much more than going it alone.

References:

Dianna Podmoroff, Mind Tools

Chew, Lillian (July 1996). Managing Derivative Risks: The Use and Abuse of Leverage. John Wiley & Sons.

Lots, Leverage, and Profit and Loss". www.babypips.com.

# Time

## Relationship With Status And Power

Time can be used as an indicator of status. For example, in most companies the boss can interrupt any one to hold an impromptu meeting in the middle of the work day, yet the average worker would have to make an appointment to see the boss. The way different cultures perceive time can influence communication as well.

Time has a definite relationship to power. Though power most often refers to the ability to influence people power is also related to dominance and status.

In the workplace, those in a leadership or management position treat time – and by virtue of position – have their time treated differently than those who are of a lower stature position. Anderson and Bowman have identified three specific examples of how chronemics and power converge in the workplace – waiting time, talk time and work time.

## Waiting Time

Researchers Insel and Lindgren (Guerrero, DeVito & Hecht, 1999, p. 325) write that the act of making an individual of a lower stature wait is a sign of dominance. They note that one who "is in the position to cause another to wait has power over him. To be kept waiting is to imply that one's time is less valuable than that of the one who imposes the wait."

Employees of equal stature will not worry about whether they are running a few minutes behind schedule to meet with one another. On the other hand, for a mid-level manager who has a meeting with the company president, a late arrival might be a nonverbal cue that you do not respect the authority of your superior.

## Talk Time

There is a direct correlation between the power of an individual in an organization and conversation. This includes both length of conversation, turn-taking and who initiates and ends a conversation. Extensive research indicates that those with more power in an organization will speak more often and for a greater length of time.

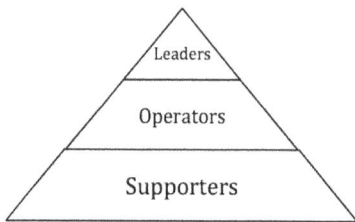

Meetings between superiors and subordinates provide an opportunity to illustrate this concept. A superior – regardless of whether or not they are running the actual meeting – lead discussions, ask questions and have the ability to speak for longer periods of time without interruption.

Likewise, research shows that turn-taking is also influenced by power. Social psychologist Nancy Henley notes that "Subordinates are expected to yield to superiors and there is a cultural expectation that a subordinate will not interrupt a superior" (Guerrero, DeVito & Hecht, 1999, p. 326).

The length of response follows the same pattern. While the superior can speak for as long as they want, the responses of the subordinate are shorter in length. Albert Mehrabian noted that deviation from this pattern led to negative perceptions of the subordinate by the superior.

Beginning and ending a communication interaction in the workplace is also controlled by the higher-status individual in an organization. The time and duration of the conversation are dictated by the higher-status individual.

## Work Time

It is not likely that you will ever see a president or a high level executive punching a time clock. Their time is perceived as more valuable and they control their own time. On the other hand, a subordinate with less power has their time controlled by a higher status individual and are in less control of their time – making them likely to report their time to a higher authority.

Such practices are more associated with those in non-supervisory roles or in blue collar rather than white collar professions. Instead, as power and status in an organization increases, the flexibility of the work schedule also increases. For instance, while administrative professionals might keep a 9 to 5 work schedule, their superiors may keep less structured hours.

This does not mean that the superior works less. They may work longer, but the structure of their work environment is not strictly dictated by the traditional work day. Instead, as Koehler and their associates note "individuals who spend more time, especially spare time, to meetings, to committees, and to developing contacts, are more likely to be influential decision makers" (Guerrero, DeVito & Hecht, 1999, p. 327).

A specific example of the way power is expressed through work time is scheduling. As Yakura and others have noted in research shared by Ballard and Seibold, "scheduling reflects the extent to which the sequencing and duration of plans activities and events are formalized" (Ballard and Seibold, p. 6). Higher-status individuals have very precise and formal schedules – indicating that their stature requires that they have specific blocks of time for specific meetings, projects and appointments.

Lower status individuals however, may have less formalized schedules. Finally, the schedule and appointment calendar of the higher status individual will take precedence in determining where, when and the importance of a specific event or appointment.

## The Triage Technique

A technique that has been proved to help prioritise the workload effectively is the Triage Technique. It is a technique that was developed during the Napoleonic years to treat wounded soldiers. Wounded soldiers were classified in 3 categories based on their injuries.

In the first category, soldiers were likely to live. In the second category soldiers were likely to die regardless of the care they could receive and finally the third category was for soldiers where immediate care was likely to make a difference. This technique helped in saving lives and proved to be much more efficient that if soldiers would have been treated on first-come-first-basis.

This technique has also been used by many armies during both world wars and proved successful. Despite the fact that we cannot compare Napoleonic wars with today's workplace this technique can effectively be applied to your work life.

You can use the Triage Technique to classify your tasks into the following 3 lines:

**1. Things that are important but not urgent**

An example would be resolving a minor issue in the office that can be resolved easily. This should be in your priority list and should be resolved at the first available opportunity. You should try to get it done by a specific time before it becomes a bigger problem.

**2. Things that are a lost cause or a waste of time**

An example would be an old photocopy machine that keeps breaking in the office. The best thing would be to get a new one right away instead of wasting your time and effort.

**3. Things that require immediate action for a positive development**

An example would be coaching an under-performing employee so that he goes back to performing at its best.

**Conclusion**

It is very important to be able to "classify" your tasks so that you are able to give them the solutions they need. This will have a positive impact on the way you work and will influence your productivity. What will allow you to become effective will be your ability to assess different tasks and situations and be able to take the actions needed to resolve them.

The triage technique offers a very efficient way to manage your tasks and become effective in the workplace. Try it now and you should rapidly see a difference in the way you work and how you will be perceived by others!

Reference:

Iserson KV, Moskop JC (March 2007). "Triage in medicine, part I: Concept, history, and types

http://www.evoliatraining.co.uk

Merriam-Webster Online Dictionary

# Action Programs

## Becoming Exceptionally Well Organized

Bringing focus to the way you work.

We all know how useful To-Do Lists are when we get started in our careers.

However, To-Do Lists can quickly become overwhelmed when we take on responsibility for multiple projects – as many of us do when we become managers.

One of the problems is that, for most of us, our To-Do Lists are not planned, focused, action lists. Rather, they are a sort of a catch-all for a lot of things that are unresolved and not yet translated into outcomes. For instance, specific entries, such as "Call Tina in Sales," might exist along with vaguer aspirations, such as "Write

marketing plan." Often, the real actionable details of what you have "to do" are missing.

Another problem is that once you have more than, say, 20 entries on your list, it becomes cumbersome and difficult to use. This means that you start missing key activities and commitments.

### Evolution of To-Do Lists

This is where Action Programs are useful. Action Programs are "industrial strength" versions of To-Do Lists, which incorporate short-, medium- and long-term goals. They help you to plan your time, without forgotten commitments coming in to blow your schedule apart. And, because they encourage you to think about your priorities properly, you can focus on the things that matter, and avoid frittering your time away on low value activities.

Actions Programs also help you get into the habit of delegating jobs. All of this lets you save time – and get away on time – whilst also increasing your effectiveness and productivity. As such, they help you bring intelligent prioritization and control back to your life, at times where you would otherwise feel overwhelmed by work.

When you first hear about them, Action Programs can sound complicated and difficult to use. They are more complicated than To-Do Lists , but if you persist and spend a few hours learning how to use them, you'll quickly find yourself back in control of your workload – and a whole lot less stressed as a result!

### How to Use an Action Program

Follow these four steps to create your Action Program:

### Step 1: Collection

First, make a long list of all the things in your world that require resolution. Try to collect and write down everything that you feel is incomplete and needs action from you to get completed, whether it's urgent or not, big or small, personal or professional.

To an extent, this collection is taking place automatically. E-mail requests are getting stored in your inbox, memos demanding attention are being delivered to your in-tray, mail is reaching your mailbox, and messages asking for action are accumulating on your voice mail.

But there is also other stuff – stuff that is idling in your head, projects you want to run, things you intend to deal with lying at the bottom of the drawer, ideas written down on stray bits of paper – that need to be gathered and put in place too. Bring all of these actions and projects together and inventory them in one place.

And – this is really important – make sure that your personal goals are brought onto this list.

You can experience tremendous stress if you have too many mental "To Dos" floating around in your head. You never know whether you've forgotten things, and you'll always have that terrible feeling of not having achieved everything you want to achieve.

By writing everything down on your Action Program, you can empty your mind of these stressful reminders and make sure that you prioritize these actions coherently and consistently. This has the incidental benefit of helping you improve your concentration, simply because you don't have these distractions buzzing around your mind.

**KEEP CALM AND Organize**

The first time you create your Action Program, you're going to spend a while – maybe two hours – putting it together. This is the up-front cost of organizing your life. However, once you've done this, you'll be amazed at how much more in control you feel. It will take relatively little effort to keep your Action Program up-to-date after this.

You'll find it easiest if you keep your Action Program on your computer as a word processor document. This will make it easy to put together, update, and maintain without a lot of tedious redrafting.

### Step 2: Pruning

Now, process the list you made in step 1, by looking carefully at each item. Decide whether you should, actually, take action on it. A lot of what comes our way has no real relevance to us, or is really not important in the scale of things. If that is the case, then delete these things from your list.

### Step 3: Organizing and Prioritizing

This step comes in three parts.

**First of all,** review your inventory of projects and actions. Group together the separate, individual actions that are part of larger projects.

At home, for example, you may want to improve your bathroom and repaint your living room: these can go into a "Home Renovation" project. At work, you may be contributing to the requirements for a new computer system, and may be expected to test and train your team on this system: all of these go into a "Computer System Upgrade" project.

What you'll find is that once you start sorting list items, they will almost seem to "organize themselves" into coherent projects. (You also need to make sure that your personal goals are included as individual projects.)

**Second,** review these projects and prioritize them in order of importance (for example, by coding them from A to F) depending on their importance. (Clearly, your personal goals are exceptionally important projects!)

**Third,** insert your projects into your Action Program (using the approach we describe below). The Action Program is split up into these three parts:

• Next Action List – this shows the small next actions that you will take to move your projects forward.

• Delegated Actions List – this shows projects and actions that you have delegated to other people.

• Project Catalog – this shows all of the projects that you are engaged in, and the small individual tasks that contribute to them.

The great news is that, by this stage, you've already created the largest part of your Action Program: the Project Catalog! This is the list of prioritized projects and activities that you've just completed.

Typically, the Project Catalog is at the back of the Action Program, as you often only have to refer to it during a weekly review process.

Next, create the Delegated Actions List by working through your Project Catalog, and identifying tasks that you've delegated. Record these under the name of the person to whom you've delegated the activity, along with the checkpoints you've agreed.

### Step 4: "Working" Your Action Program

An Action Program is typically fairly long. But you don't have to run through the entire Program every day!

> *Once in India, Prabhupada was joined in his room by his senior disciples Bhagavan, Brahmananda and Giriraja. "You are the future hope of the world," said Srila Prabhupada, and he began to instruct them about the importance of proper organization. "Just like your American Express corporation," he said. "What have they done? They have simply taken pieces of paper and for those pieces of paper you pay good money. But what have they done? Actually they have done nothing. It is simply management. You pay them some money and they give you a piece of paper, and if you lose that piece of paper, they say, 'All right, we will give you another piece of paper.' It is organization. Simply from that management they have made millions of dollars."*
>
> *~ Srila Prabhupada Nectar*

Usually, you'll only be dealing with the top page or pages, which are your Next Actions list and your Delegated Actions list. Some activities may be day-specific or time-specific. Depending of the way you work, you can either maintain these on the top page of your Action Program, or mark them in your calendar.

In effect, these top pages are just a new form of your old To-Do List. It's just that only specific short actions are outlined here, while the major projects to which the actions belong are stored in your Project Catalog.

What you must do, however, is review and update your Action Program periodically, for example, every week (put time for this in your schedule). Delete or archive items you've completed, move items from the Project Catalog to the front pages as you make progress on your projects, and add any new actions that have come your way.

Reference:

Dianna Podmoroff , mindtools, Time Management

Mark Forster in his book "Do It Tomorrow and Other Secrets of Time Management".

Brian Tracy, Time Management: How You Can Become Action Oriented

## Personal SWOT Analysis

### Making the Most of Your Talents and Opportunities

And Your Strengths And Weaknesses

Chance favors the prepared mind.– Louis Pasteur

A SWOT matrix is a framework for analyzing your strengths and weaknesses as well as the opportunities and threats that you face. This helps you focus on your strengths, minimize your weaknesses, and take the greatest possible advantage of opportunities available to you.

You are most likely to succeed in life if you use your talents to their fullest extent.

Similarly, you'll suffer fewer problems if you know what your weaknesses are, and if you manage these weaknesses so that they don't matter in the work you do.

So how you go about identifying these strengths and weaknesses, and analyzing the opportunities and threats that flow from them? SWOT Analysis is a useful technique that helps you do this.

What makes SWOT especially powerful is that, with a little thought, it can help you uncover opportunities that you would not otherwise have spotted. And by understanding your weaknesses, you can manage and eliminate threats that might otherwise hurt your ability to move forward.

If you look at yourself using the SWOT framework, you can start to separate yourself from your peers, and further develop the specialized talents and abilities you need to advance in your life.

## How to Use the Tool

To perform a personal SWOT analysis, write down answers to the following questions.

### Strengths

• What advantages do you have that others don't have (for example, skills, certifications, education, or connections)?
• What do you do better than anyone else?
• What personal resources can you access?
• What do other people (and your boss, in particular) see as your strengths?
• Which of your achievements are you most proud of?
• What values do you believe in that others fail to exhibit?

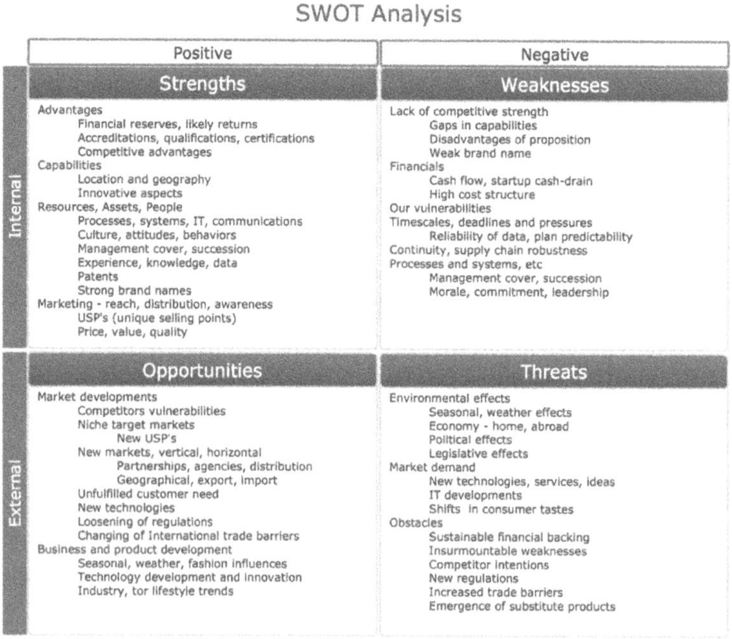

## SWOT Analysis

| Positive | Negative |
|---|---|
| **Strengths** | **Weaknesses** |
| Advantages<br>  Financial reserves, likely returns<br>  Accreditations, qualifications, certifications<br>  Competitive advantages<br>Capabilities<br>  Location and geography<br>  Innovative aspects<br>Resources, Assets, People<br>  Processes, systems, IT, communications<br>  Culture, attitudes, behaviors<br>  Management cover, succession<br>  Experience, knowledge, data<br>  Patents<br>  Strong brand names<br>Marketing - reach, distribution, awareness<br>  USP's (unique selling points)<br>  Price, value, quality | Lack of competitive strength<br>  Gaps in capabilities<br>  Disadvantages of proposition<br>  Weak brand name<br>Financials<br>  Cash flow, startup cash-drain<br>  High cost structure<br>Our vulnerabilities<br>Timescales, deadlines and pressures<br>  Reliability of data, plan predictability<br>Continuity, supply chain robustness<br>Processes and systems, etc<br>  Management cover, succession<br>  Morale, commitment, leadership |
| **Opportunities** | **Threats** |
| Market developments<br>  Competitors vulnerabilities<br>  Niche target markets<br>    New USP's<br>  New markets, vertical, horizontal<br>    Partnerships, agencies, distribution<br>    Geographical, export, import<br>  Unfulfilled customer need<br>  New technologies<br>  Loosening of regulations<br>  Changing of international trade barriers<br>Business and product development<br>  Seasonal, weather, fashion influences<br>  Technology development and innovation<br>  Industry, tor lifestyle trends | Environmental effects<br>  Seasonal, weather effects<br>  Economy - home, abroad<br>  Political effects<br>  Legislative effects<br>Market demand<br>  New technologies, services, ideas<br>  IT developments<br>  Shifts in consumer tastes<br>Obstacles<br>  Sustainable financial backing<br>  Insurmountable weaknesses<br>  Competitor intentions<br>  New regulations<br>  Increased trade barriers<br>  Emergence of substitute products |

(Internal / External rows as labeled)

- Are you part of a network that no one else is involved in? If so, what connections do you have with influential people?

Consider this from your own perspective, and from the point of view of the people around you. And don't be modest or shy – be as objective as you can.

And if you have any difficulty with this, write down a list of your personal characteristics. Some of these will hopefully be strengths!

### Weaknesses

- What tasks do you usually avoid because you don't feel confident doing them?
- What will the people around you see as your weaknesses?
- Are you completely confident in your education and skills training? If not, where are you weakest?
- What are your negative work habits (for example, are you often late, are you disorganized, do you have a short temper, or are you poor at handling stress)?
- Do you have personality traits that hold you back in your field? For instance, if you have to conduct meetings on a regular basis, a fear of public speaking would be a major weakness.

Again, consider this from a personal/internal perspective and an external perspective. Do other people see weaknesses that you don't see? Do co-workers consistently outperform you in key areas? Be realistic – it's best to face any unpleasant truths as soon as possible.

### Opportunities

- What new technology can help you? Or can you get help from others or from people via the Internet?
- Is your industry growing? If so, how can you take advantage of the current market?
- Do you have a network of strategic contacts to help you, or offer good advice?
- What trends (management or otherwise) do you see in your company, and how can you take advantage of them?
- Are any of your competitors failing to do something important? If so, can you take advantage of their mistakes?

• Is there a need in your company or industry that no one is filling?

• Do your customers or vendors complain about something in your company? If so, could you create an opportunity by offering a solution?

You might find useful opportunities in the following:

• Networking events, educational classes, or conferences.

• A colleague going on an extended leave. Could you take on some of this person's projects to gain experience?

• A new role or project that forces you to learn new skills, like public speaking or international relations.

• A company expansion or acquisition. Do you have specific skills (like a second language) that could help with the process?

Also, importantly, look at your strengths, and ask yourself whether these open up any opportunities – and look at your weaknesses, and ask yourself whether you could open up opportunities by eliminating those weaknesses.

### Threats

• What obstacles do you currently face at work?

• Are any of your colleagues competing with you for projects or roles?

• Is your job (or the demand for the things you do) changing?

• Does changing technology threaten your position?

• Could any of your weaknesses lead to threats?

Performing this analysis will often provide key information – it can point out what needs to be done and put problems into perspective.

### A Personal SWOT Example

What would a personal SWOT assessment look like? Review this SWOT analysis for Carol, an advertising manager.

### Strengths

• I'm very creative. I often impress clients with a new perspective on their brands.

- I communicate well with my clients and team.
- I have the ability to ask key questions to find just the right marketing angle.
- I'm completely committed to the success of a client's brand.

Weaknesses
- I have a strong, compulsive need to do things quickly and remove them from my "to do" list, and sometimes the quality of my work suffers as a result.
- This same need to get things done also causes me stress when I have too many tasks.
- I get nervous when presenting ideas to clients, and this fear of public speaking often takes the passion out of my presentations.

Opportunities
- One of our major competitors has developed a reputation for treating their smaller clients poorly.
- I'm attending a major marketing conference next month. This will allow for strategic networking, and also offer some great training seminars.
- Our art director will go on maternity leave soon. Covering her duties while she's away would be a great career development opportunity for me.

Threats
- Raghu, one of my colleagues, is a much stronger speaker than I am, and he's competing with me for the art director position.
- Due to recent staff shortages, I'm often overworked, and this negatively impacts my creativity.
- The current economic climate has resulted in slow growth for the marketing industry. Many firms have laid off staff members, and our company is considering further cutbacks.

References
Chad Brooks, Nov 2013, www.businessnewsdaily.com
Humphrey, Albert (December 2005). "SWOT Analysis for Management Consulting".
SRI Alumni Newsletter (SRI International).
Hill, T. & R. Westbrook (1997). "SWOT Analysis: It's Time for a Product Recall".

# THE AUTHOR

Dr. Sahadeva dasa (Sanjay Shah) is a monk in vaisnava tradition. His areas of work include research in Vedic and contemporary thought, Corporate and educational training, social work and counselling, travelling, writing books and of course, practicing spiritual life and spreading awareness about the same.

He is also an accomplished musician, composer, singer, instruments player and sound engineer. He has more than a dozen albums to his credit so far. (SoulMelodies.com)

His varied interests include alternative holistic living, Vedic studies, social criticism, environment, linguistics, history, art & crafts, nature studies, web technologies etc.

Many of his books have been acclaimed internationally and translated in other languages.

# By The Same Author

*Oil-Final Countdown To A Global Crisis And Its Solutions*

*End of Modern Civilization And Alternative Future*

*To Kill Cow Means To End Human Civilization*

*Cow And Humanity - Made For Each Other*

*Cows Are Cool - Love 'Em!*

*Let's Be Friends - A Curious, Calm Cow*

*Wondrous Glories of Vraja*

*We Feel Just Like You Do*

*Tsunami Of Diseases Headed Our Way - Know Your Food Before Time Runs Out*

*Cow Killing And Beef Export - The Master Plan To Turn India Into A Desert By 2050*

*Capitalism Communism And Cowism - A New Economics For The 21st Century*

*Noble Cow - Munching Grass, Looking Curious And Just Hanging Around*

*World - Through The Eyes Of Scriptures*

*To Save Time Is To Lengthen Life*

*Life Is Nothing But Time - Time Is Life, Life Is Time*

*An Inch of Time Can Not Be Bought With A Mile of Gold*

*Spare Us Some Carcasses - An Appeal From The Vultures*

*Cow Dung - A Down-To- Earth Solution To Global Warming And Climate Change*

*Cow Dung For Food Security And Survival of Human Race*

(More information on availability on DrDasa.com )

www.ingramcontent.com/pod-product-compliance
Lightning Source LLC
Chambersburg PA
CBHW070641030426
42337CB00020B/4105